The Human Dimension:
Experiences in Policy Research

by

HADLEY CANTRIL

Rutgers University Press

New Brunswick   *New Jersey*

Copyright © 1967 by Rutgers, The State University
Library of Congress Catalogue Card Number: 66-25173
Printed in the United States of America
by Quinn & Boden Company, Inc., Rahway, New Jersey

Permission to quote from *The Politics of Despair*, by Hadley
Cantril, © 1958 by Basic Books, Inc., Publishers, New York, has
been kindly granted by Basic Books.

To
JERRY LAMBERT

Contents

Preface

I recount here some of my attempts to inject a way of thinking into policy formulation at the highest levels of Government. This "way of thinking" consists essentially in using all necessary psychological factors in the formulation of any given problem. For only if the psychological dimensions of policy are taken into account in advance can there be any assurance that both policy planning and the actions based on policy decisions will not be thwarted by obstacles that could be obviated by properly designed research.

Through a process of serendipity recounted later, I happened to be propelled into policy research for Franklin D. Roosevelt during World War II. I also served as special consultant to the White House for a while during the Eisenhower Administration and on a few occasions worked with the Kennedy Administration. At no time was I ever a paid member of any Government staff. But I am eager not to give the impression that my relationship with occupants of the White House was especially intimate, for many social scientists have worked closer than I ever did, but none, I believe, as a psychologist with a similar purpose. Throughout all my Washington activities, I tried to avoid any publicity about them.

I had originally intended to write up some examples of my experiences in policy research and have them published posthumously, since it seemed inappropriate to report such incidents during my lifetime. But a number of people to whom I have shown the reports of this research have urged me to publish them. In spite of the millions of dollars spent by Government and private sources for social science research of one kind or another, there actually is still very little such research initiated or even utilized by those most responsible for Government policies on either the domestic or foreign fronts. The whole concept of research concerned with the psychological and political dynamics of people simply has not yet been effectively geared into the United States Government operation.

I should hasten to add that this state of affairs is by no means entirely the fault of Government officials. All too many social scientists, including psychologists, have been satisfied to spend their lives conducting research that is concerned either with theory or technique only, much of which assumes the character of playing games or building models that will impress their peers. Obviously such research can be of importance to the development of the social sciences, but most of it unfortunately has very little demonstrated relevance to the decisions which policy makers must reach, and it is little wonder that they become impatient with it. The scarcity of the type of research I am describing here is a major reason for publishing now a sample of the studies I have made over the past twenty-five years.

Because the book includes some studies I made in my role as a practitioner, I have presented them in the simple, anecdotal language of an empiricist, with the thought that these may provide some clues to an art of investigation usable long after I and those who speak my professional vocabulary are dead and gone. Such a permanent record may encourage younger social scientists to do better. And it may confirm for responsible officials the potential value of this kind of thinking and research, not in order to help determine broad objectives of Government policy, but to help implement effectively the objectives decided on. By discovering where people are ignorant, unconcerned, or resistant, one can educate them in the problems of modern government and thus enable them to become more constructively critical. Clearly, democracy requires effective, reliable two-way communication between the governing and the governed.

Studies such as those described here could, of course, be misused by those in power or those who aspire to power by pandering in irresponsible ways to public opinion or to the deep aspirations men and women feel and express. Fortunately, the American people have by now, I think, developed sufficient sensitivity to be able to recognize attempts to exploit their feelings purely for political gain and are quick to discount the glib generalizations of those who overpromise and overpromote.

I begin the story with an account of two relatively recent studies done by our Institute for International Social Research in Cuba and in the Dominican Republic, which show how policy research could anticipate a crisis in time for it to be averted or at least mitigated. Then I consider the theory behind such research and the tools used. The major portion of the book gives some illustrations of different types of policy research: discovering and reporting the state of mind of people, learning how aware they are of issues that require policy decisions and how research can help to find the right expression of policy at the right time so as to reach the people more effectively. The final chapter delineates the problem of injecting psychological considerations into Government policy.

HADLEY CANTRIL

Princeton, New Jersey
March 1966

Acknowledgements

The book is dedicated to my dear friend, Gerard B. Lambert, one of the few really brilliant men it has been my good fortune to know well. Jerry was a most imaginative and creative partner in much of the work done for Roosevelt during the war, and his generous financial aid made it possible for me to conduct any research for Roosevelt I wanted without ever having to depend on or accept Government funds of any kind.

I should also acknowledge the faithful assistance of Elizabeth V. Deyo, my able executive secretary during so many of the years this research was going on, who prepared all the then-confidential reports sent to the White House and to Military Intelligence. I am most grateful to Alice Anne Navin for her editorial assistance.

HADLEY CANTRIL

The Human Dimension:
Experiences in Policy Research

1

Castro's Popularity at Home

The studies reported in this and the next chapter show how a bit of pertinent research can anticipate problems that should affect policy decisions at the highest level. Both studies were done by the Institute for International Social Research and were directed and reported by my associate Lloyd Free. Despite their wide circulation among top policy makers, both seem to have been buried until after major decisions were forced on President Kennedy in the first case and President Johnson in the second, when the relevance of the findings to the situation that emerged was belatedly recognized. These two studies illustrate in a nutshell the possibilities of policy research based on a way of thinking and a technique that can be utilized simply, informally, and inexpensively; they are neglected at the cost of American substance, lives, prestige, and confidence.

During April and May 1960, a little more than a year after Castro took over in Cuba and just about a year before the invasion attempt, Free conducted a survey in Cuba to determine what the opinions of Cubans were toward the Castro regime. The study is one in a series made by Lloyd on the dynamics of political behavior.[1]

As might be expected, arranging for and executing this study presented unusual difficulties because of the political climate in Cuba at the time. Lloyd had trouble finding a competent Cuban research organization willing to undertake the assignment. The organizations he had counted on originally to do the job backed out at the last minute, particularly after an informal inquiry of a high official in the Cuban Government elicited the reply that conducting such a survey would be "suicidal" under the circumstances. The men in charge of the organization that finally agreed to take the assignment did so because they felt they had already burned so many bridges behind them that one more wouldn't really matter. Lloyd made arrangements with them in Havana and himself interviewed a number of Cuban élite. Those who managed the study have long since left Cuba.

The sample on which the results were based represented a cross-section of the urban and semi-urban population, which constituted about 60 per cent of the population of Cuba. One thousand people were interviewed. It proved impossible to interview the inhabitants of rural areas because their suspiciousness had been so intensified by the political climate of Revolutionary Cuba. The study also, of course, could not include any direct questions and utilized entirely what technicians call open-ended questions, questions worded indirectly in such a way that very few people would refuse to answer them.

Whatever the opinions of outside observers about trends in Cuba, at the time of our survey the Cuban people were highly optimistic about future progress, both personal and national, if only because of what they conceived to be vast improvement over the days of Batista.

The thousand Cubans interviewed in Havana and other cities, in towns and villages throughout the island, were first questioned about their personal hopes and aspirations on the one hand and their personal worries and fears on the other. They were then shown a picture of a ladder with eleven steps, ranging from zero at the bottom, which, they were told, represented the worst state of affairs their worries and fears could project, to ten at the top, representing the best state of affairs they could anticipate. Then they were asked to indicate where, in terms of their own personal lives, they stood on the ladder, where they had stood five years before, and where they thought they would stand five years in the future. The average ratings that emerged showed an optimistic continuum from past to present to future: moving from a rating of 4.1 for five years ago, through 6.3 for the present, and up to 8.4 for five years ahead.[2]

After they had been similarly questioned about their hopes and aspirations, worries and fears in connection with their country, people were asked to indicate where they thought Cuba then stood on the ladder, where it had stood five years before, and where they thought it would stand five years in the future. The average national ratings show an even sharper rise in optimistic directions than did the personal, particularly in terms of progress from Batista's Cuba, which they rated very low, to the Cuba of 1960. Here the average rating for the past for Cuba was only 2.1, jumping to 6.9 for the present under Castro, and moving up to 8.8 for the future. Thus, the prevailing mood of the great majority of Cubans in April and May 1960 was one of hope and optimism.

Eighty-six per cent of the people in this sample of the urban population expressed themselves in favor of the Castro regime and the situation in Cuba at the time. Only about one out of every ten urban Cubans could be described as a dedicated opponent of Castro. And there is no reason to believe that any less support for the Revolution and for Fidel Castro would have been found among rural people if they could have been interviewed. As was to be expected, a higher percentage of Castro supporters was found among the younger elements than among the older; among people living outside Havana (93 per cent) than among the residents of that metropolis (72 per cent); among those with elementary or no schooling (90 per cent) than among those with secondary education (83 per cent) or university training (77 per cent); among the lowest socio-economic groups (90 per cent) than among the lower-middle (87 per cent) and particularly the upper and upper-middle group (71 per cent).

When people were asked to indicate what their fears and worries were for the future of the country, the chief concern, expressed by 30 per cent, was that Cuba would return to past conditions of tyranny, dictatorship, oppression; that there would be a counterrevolution or take-over by another dictator or tyrant. So long as the only alternative to Castro appeared to be another Batista, and the only alternative to the situation at the time appeared to be something resembling the past, there was no likelihood that any shift would take place in the overwhelming allegiance to Castro, even if economic conditions should deteriorate.

Lloyd Free's report on Cuba, published in July of 1960, was, like all his reports, distributed to the White House, the State Department, and the United States Information Agency, and through the State Department to many other Government departments and agencies, and to academic scholars. Copies went to newspapers and to various interested individuals on our mailing list. Around 500 copies had been sent out within a month of publication. On August 2 the *New York Times* carried a rather full account of the major findings, and our Institute promptly filled a request for a dozen copies from the Cuban Embassy in Washington.

It should be noted that it was during the last months of

the Eisenhower Administration that the report was disseminated to Government agencies. It would appear that it was buried or forgotten after the 1960 Presidential election. Shortly after the ill-fated invasion attempt, a copy of the report was sent to Arthur Schlesinger, Jr., who was then serving as a Special Assistant to President Kennedy. In his note of acknowledgment to Lloyd, Mr. Schlesinger wrote: "I read with interest your Cuban report—and only wish that a copy had come to my attention earlier."

This study on Cuba showed unequivocally not only that the great majority of Cubans supported Castro, but that any hope of stimulating action against him or exploiting a powerful opposition in connection with the United States invasion of 1961 was completely chimerical, no matter what Cuban exiles said or felt about the situation, and that the fiasco and its aftermath, in which the United States became involved, was predictable.

2

1962: Trouble Ahead in Santo Domingo

In April of 1965, the attempt of the so-called rebel forces to restore constitutional government and return Juan Bosch to the Presidency set off bloody fighting in Santo Domingo and caused President Johnson to order American troops to that city, not only to protect American lives, but, presumably, to keep the rebel movement out of the hands of Communists and prevent another Cuba. The Organization of American States then sent other forces to join those of the United States in trying to establish a cease-fire between the opposing forces. A three-man peace committee sent to the Dominican Republic by the Organization of American States managed to get the contending parties to agree to a provisional government in September 1965, after about four months of intermittent civil war. Peace was finally restored.

The study described here was made during the spring of 1962, about a year after the political assassination of the dictator, Rafael L. Trujillo, who had ruthlessly ruled that benighted land for over three decades. Six months after the report was issued, Juan Bosch was elected President in the first free election held in the Dominican Republic in thirty-eight years. After seven months in power, Bosch was overthrown in a military coup; a three-man civilian junta, backed by the military, took over the government, and Bosch retired to Puerto Rico.

The report is based on a public opinion survey conducted on a cross-section of over 800 adults in the Dominican Republic during April 1962. It shows, in brief, the extreme frustration of the Dominican people: the wide gap between their situation at the time and what they wanted out of life, always a sign of trouble ahead if the gap is not narrowed or if there seems no real hope that it will be narrowed in the immediate future. At the same time, we see from this report how extremely pro-United States, anti-Communist, and anti-Castro the Dominican people were at the time.

I am paraphrasing the report as it was issued in 1962 and am quoting a few key passages that were written into the record and distributed to many people in the Government.[3]

What were the unrequited needs, desires, and hopes of the Dominican people? What were their principal worries, fears, and preoccupations?

To get at these matters at the personal level, we asked the following two questions: "All of us want certain things out of life. When you think about what really matters in your own life, what are your wishes and hopes for the future? In other words, if you imagine your future in the best possible light, what would your life look like then if you are to be happy?" Then, "Now imagine the contrary. If you picture your future in the worst possible light, what would your life look like then? In other words, what are your worries and fears about the future?"

By far the chief personal aspiration of the Dominican people, mentioned by 72 per cent, was their desire for a better standard of living. Then came the desire to own their own house, mentioned by 55 per cent. Approximately 25 per cent indicated their wish to have their own land or farm, steady or congenial work, and opportunities for their children. The chief personal worries people expressed were the reverse of their hopes: 76 per cent were concerned about a possible deterioration in their standard of living and 24 per cent were afraid of unemployment.

Whether expressed as aspirations or as worries and fears, these personal preoccupations of the Dominicans demonstrated the potential appeal of political platforms or programs having to do with housing, landownership, employment, public health, and education. But the big thing in the Dominican mind was the desire for an improved standard of living, often from the elemental level of sheer hunger, expressed both in their aspiration and their fear with a frequency never encountered in the studies our Institute has completed to date.

"Since I am so poor, I need a house and some money, because I am suffering terrible hunger. There are days when we don't even eat at all here for lack of ways of getting money." (A fifty-seven-year-old farmer.)

"If I don't get economic aid soon, I don't know what I shall do, because these three children of mine are going to fall dead from hunger." (A twenty-five-year-old female pensioner.)

"I should like to have enough food for my children. If I had this, I would feel happy with my life." (A twenty-three-year-old housewife.)

The frustration of the Dominican people because of their low standard of living is further borne out by the concerns they expressed for their nation. The questions asked were: "Now, what are your wishes and hopes for the future of our country? If you picture the future of the Dominican Republic in the best possible light, how would things look, let us say, about ten years from now?" Then, "Considering now the other side of the picture, what are your fears and worries for the future of our country? If you picture the future of the Dominican Republic in the worst possible light, how would things look about ten years from now?"

Again, as with personal concerns, the most frequently mentioned aspiration, indicated by 67 per cent, was for a decent standard of living, with 42 per cent wishing for jobs for everyone. Second on the list was the hope for political stability and internal peace and order, mentioned by 58 per cent, with 26 per cent specifically stating their desire for efficient government and competent leadership. As to their fears for the nation, political instability, chaos, and war led the list by far, with 49 per cent expressing concern about these. Fear of Communism and its consequences was explicitly mentioned by 22 per cent. Fear that there would be no improvement in their standard of living was expressed by 27 per cent.

Clearly, the so-called revolution in rising expectations had taken hold with a vengeance among the Dominican people, as was evident from the large percentages who referred to economic betterment as a *personal* aspiration. Beyond this, however, two-thirds of the sample—the highest proportion ever recorded in our research to date—expressed the desire for an improved standard of living as a *national* problem involving the Dominican people as a whole, rather than as a strictly personal or family problem. The revolution in rising expectations had surely taken hold in the Dominican Republic in a form which had *political* meaning for the society as a whole. Lloyd Free wrote in his report that "the Dominicans appear to view economic betterment as a national, political problem to be solved by the Dominican Government—or else. This high degree of political awareness, in itself, constitutes a potentially explosive factor in an already surcharged situation."

To find out how the people thought the country was doing under present circumstances, our sample was asked the following question: "Here is a ladder (the steps of which are numbered from zero at the bottom to ten at the top). Let's suppose the top of the ladder represents the very best situation for our country, as you have just described it; and the bottom the very worst situation for our country. Please show me on which step of the ladder you think the Dominican Republic is at the present time. Where was it five years ago? Just as your best guess, on which step do you think our country will be about five years from now?"

The average past rating for the country was only 1.7, the rating for the present moved up only to 2.7, while that for the future jumped dramatically to 7.0. The past rating (for the Republic under Trujillo) was the lowest any people have ever assigned their country in the surveys we have done to date—even lower than the Cubans gave to the Cuba of Batista in the survey carried out a year after Castro took over (2.2).

The rise from 1.7 for the past to 2.7 for the present indicated some sense of national progress, to be sure, which, incidentally, proved to be much more marked among the upper socio-economic groups and the urbanites than among the lower groups and those living in rural areas. However, this jump of only 1.0 point from past to present was by no means what might have been expected of a people who had just emerged from thirty years of oppressive dictatorship. In contrast, the Cuban figures reported in the first chapter went up from 2.2 for the Cuba of Batista to 7.0 for the Cuba of Castro, a rise of 4.8 points. On top of the modestness of the increment, the fact is that the rating assigned the Dominican Republic as of 1962 (2.7) was the lowest rating for the present we have ever encountered in our surveys.

But, low as the national ratings were for past and present, the real shocker emerged when the Dominicans were asked to use the ladder to indicate where they personally stood five years ago, where they stood at the time of the study, and where they thought they would stand five years ahead. Here the average personal rating for five years ago was a mere 1.6, the average present rating was exactly the same, 1.6, but the future rating was 5.8.

Clearly, the Dominicans as a whole had absolutely no sense of personal progress from past to present. While the urbanites and upper socio-economic groups tended to feel that they were somewhat better off than under Trujillo, the prevailing opinion among the masses was that there had been no change for the better. The Dominicans obviously felt they were very badly off in absolute terms: *no less than one-third of the sample assigned themselves, in terms of their personal lives, the lowest possible score of zero.*

The intensity of this evident frustration must have been contributed to by the widespread expectations that the overthrow of Trujillo would usher in the era of the promised land. This surge in expectations only made the situation of relative anarchy and misery seem even worse than it really was. Whatever all the factors may be that were involved, "we feel confident in alleging that *an extremely serious situation of popular discontent and frustration, fraught with a dangerous potential for upheaval, exists in the Dominican Republic.* Never have we seen the danger signals so unmistakably clear." (Italics were in original report.)

That there was still some time available was evident from the optimism shown in the high figures the Dominicans assigned themselves and their country in their ratings of the future. In their view, there still appeared to be hope. But with the situation in 1962 so largely unstructured and popular frustration already so highly banked, almost anything could happen, including shifts in the attitudes at the time, which were favorable to the United States and opposed to

Communism and Castroism. In the words of a thirty-five-year-old Dominican domestic worker:

"My fears and worries for the future are: that we fail to live in peace and tranquility; that if the future should be worse than now, there will be still more misery and hunger and no sources of work; *that we shall suffer the same fate as Cuba.*"

The United States was enormously popular with the Dominican people. In asking our cross-section to indicate their opinion of the United States, we used our ladder scaling device. With 10.0 as the optimum possible score, the Dominicans gave the United States an average rating of 9.1—the highest score any people our Institute has studied so far have ever assigned a foreign country.

President Kennedy's average popularity rating was even higher: an almost unbelievable 9.4. Three-quarters of those with opinions gave him the highest possible rating of 10.0.

Asked with which countries the Dominican Republic should cooperate very closely, 75 per cent of the sample mentioned the United States, with the next highest percentage being a mere 5 per cent for Venezuela. Nor was there any question in the minds of the vast majority of Dominicans about which side their country should take in the cold war. Asked whether the Dominican Republic should side with the United States, with Russia, or with neither, 83 per cent opted for siding with America. Only 1 per cent said "Russia" and 5 per cent "neither"; the balance, amounting to 11 per cent, had no opinion. In short, neutralistic sentiments were almost entirely lacking on the Dominican scene.

Clearly, it was relations with the United States which constituted the great reality and primary frame of reference for Dominican outlooks on international affairs.

A majority of 56 per cent felt that current relations between the Dominican Republic and the United States were "very good," with another 21 per cent answering "somewhat good," and almost none thinking they verged on the bad. The main reasons given for thinking relationships were so good were that the United States had helped the Dominican Republic; had extended economic and technical assistance; had sent food and medicines—indicated by 61 per cent; the two countries have always been good friends, very close, brother countries; we Dominicans have always been able to look to the United States—indicated by 19 per cent.

One-third of the sample had "heard or read" of the "Alliance for Progress"; and among those who had, an overwhelming majority (93 per cent) were for it.

Finally, in what is held to constitute the most sincere form of flattery, a large majority of Dominicans felt that their own country should imitate the United States. The question asked was: "We are clearly entering a new era in our country's history in which there will be an opportunity to choose a new governmental system and way of life. In deciding what we should do, some people think there are lessons to be learned from the experience of other countries. Is there any particular country which comes to mind in this connection—that is, one which has a political system and way of life that you admire and would like to see followed here in the Dominican Republic?"

The United States was named by 65 per cent while the next most frequent mention—but by only 8 per cent—was Puerto Rico. One of the reasons for putting the preceding question on the ballot was to test whether the Communist, and particularly the Cuban example, had any appeal for Dominicans. Obviously, it did not. Less than one-half of 1 per cent mentioned a desire to imitate any Communist country at all (Russia), and there were no mentions whatever of Cuba. This is an accurate indication of the attitudes of Dominicans toward Castroism and Communism in general. Asked to show their opinions of Russia and of Cuba on the ladder device mentioned above, they produced an average score for Russia (as compared with a popularity rating for the United States of 9.1) of 1.0 and for Cuba, 0.6. The Cuban rating was the lowest ever assigned a foreign country among the peoples our Institute has surveyed to date.

In related vein, while President Kennedy's score was 9.4, that for Khrushchev was 1.0 and for Castro a mere 0.3, the latter reflecting the fact that 85 per cent of those with an opinion gave Castro the lowest possible score of zero.

Castro's problem in the Dominican Republic was not that he was unknown. Seven out of ten Dominicans were able to volunteer his name when asked "who is the Premier and top leader in Cuba?" An additional 16 per cent, once his name was mentioned, said they had "heard or read" of him, making a total of 87 per cent in all who said they knew of him. But he was bitterly disliked, chiefly because "he is a Communist, allied to Russia, etc." (mentioned by 56 per cent); and secondarily, because he was considered "a bad man, a killer, an assassin" (mentioned by 25 per cent).

Quite apart from Castro, the Dominicans were thoroughly skeptical of Communism in general. The question put to the people was: "If at some future time the Dominican Communists should come to power in this country, do you think they would tend to work for the best interests of the Dominican Republic and the Dominican people, or to work for the best interests of Russia and Communism?" Only 3 per cent answered that the Dominican Communists would work for the best interests of the Dominican Republic, while 86 per cent felt they would work for the best interests of Russia.

Since Lloyd and I felt the report was still most relevant to the proper solution of the Dominican problem when the crisis arose during the spring of 1965, the report was republished and again sent to a number of people in Government, including the White House and the United States representative to the Organization of American States, the Honorable Ellsworth Bunker.

On June 1, 1965, Lloyd learned that the President had read his Dominican report, that the White House had had it reproduced and distributed at the highest levels. Bill Moyers, one of President Johnson's top assistants, said it had proved "very useful." On the same day, I received a note from McGeorge Bundy, the White House assistant who had initially handled the Dominican affair for the President, acknowledging the "timely" study.

Surely if any example of policy research was neglected in the initial formulation of policy and action, it was this study of the Dominican Republic made three years before the crisis occurred, predicting the trouble ahead, and with clear implications for the stance the United States Government might have taken to preserve its good reputation with a people so eager to be friendly and so strongly anti-Communist. Obviously, a repeat study gathering the same information after the events of 1965 would be not only of interest but of great value in guiding United States policy during the crucial years ahead for the Dominican people.

3

Eisenhower and Perception Demonstrations

The studies in the Dominican Republic and in Cuba, like the other research to be reported here, are based on the theory that the way we look at things and the attitudes and opinions we form are grounded on assumptions we have learned from our experience in life. Every person must not only learn what things are, where they are, and what they are "for," but must also learn to make reliable guesses concerning the implication for him of the behavior of other people and what their probable intentions are as these might affect him. The significances a person attaches to anything, whether an object, another individual, or a symbol, are significances that he has so far found reliable in orienting himself to his environment. Even though a person may regard the assumptions he has learned as certainties, they are in the final analysis merely probabilities that he accepts on faith as long as they work.

Once assumptions are formed and prove more or less effective, they serve both to focus attention and screen out what is apparently irrelevant and, as reinforcing agents, to intensify other aspects of the environment which seem to have a direct bearing on our purposes. Thus we do not "react *to*" our environment in any simple mechanistic way but "transact *with*" an environment in which we ourselves play the role of active agent. This approach to an understanding of human behavior has therefore come to be called "transactional psychology."

I call this pattern of assumptions a person builds up and by means of which he interprets the natural and social world around him, his "assumptive world" or his "reality world." It is a world created by an individual's own participation in it. It is the only world he knows. While a person's reality world is unique to him alone, it contains, of course, many assumptions shared by others because of common experiences and backgrounds and similar purposes.[4]

The general orientation I had been pursuing since 1932 was reinforced, extended, and elaborated when in 1947 I met and began to work closely with Adelbert Ames, Jr., one of the leading men in the world in the field of physiological optics. Ames had devised a number of ingenious and exciting demonstrations in perception which illustrated the role played by the assumptions a person brings to a situation in determining the nature of the experience he will have in that situation. While I was a consultant to the White House, working with Nelson Rockefeller, then a special assistant to Eisenhower on psychological problems relating to the cold war, Nelson arranged to have me show the President some of the demonstrations in perception developed by Del Ames. Our thought was that a few of the basic points the demonstrations were designed to illustrate might be useful in the Government's attempt to influence the reactions of people in other nations to the United States and its policies. The demonstrations particularly showed how difficult it is to make people see things differently by means of any purely intellectual, argumentative approach. The obvious conclusion then is that any approach should be made in a person's own terms, from the point of view of his experience, his purposes, and his understanding of the proper means to accomplish his ends.

Accordingly, I arranged with Mr. Kimball Whipple of Hanover, New Hampshire, who had constructed all our demonstrations, to meet me in Washington on the evening of July 4, 1955. The demonstrations we had chosen to show the President were taken down from our Princeton laboratory that day. Whipple and I stayed up until early morning assembling the equipment in what is known as the Fish-Bowl Room of the White House, near the President's office. As we went about our job, we could hear the Fourth of July fireworks being set off around the Washington Monument.

I showed the demonstrations to the President the next morning. Also present were James Haggerty, press secretary, Nelson Rockefeller, General Theodore Parker, and Lloyd Free. The session quickly assumed a relaxed and informal atmosphere. I asked the President to take a seat while I first showed him the "revolving trapezoid window." This is a demonstration in which a trapezoidal shape that looks like a window frame is continuously rotated by a small motor. But to the observer, the "window" appears to oscillate back and forth. The illusion is due to the fact that we have become so used to rectangular windows that we assume the two ends of the window are the same length; hence if one edge of the window subtends a slightly larger angle on the retina we interpret it as being closer to us than the other edge. For that is the way we have experienced windows all our lives when we were not looking at them head on and when they formed a trapezoid on our retinas. The trapezoidal window is so designed that the longer edge always subtends a larger angle on the retina; hence when one looks at it, this longer edge, though moving, is never seen to go farther away from us than the shorter edge; and so we see it oscillate instead of revolve. And even after a person is shown how the illusion is created and is told the theory behind it, he still sees it oscillate back and forth when he looks at it again. His intellectual knowledge does not change his perception.

When this was finished, the President asked, "Well, doctor, what do you want me to do now?" I then had him sit in front of the "distorted room"—a room which looks quite rectangular when a person sees it from a certain vantage point with one eye, but which in reality is distorted in such a way that it produces the same image on the retina as a normal room. One of the standard procedures in this demonstration is to ask a person to "swat the fly" with a long wand held in the left hand. The "fly" is simply a black mark painted over one of the windows on the right side of the distorted room. But since the room is so constructed that the left wall is twice as long as the right wall and the back wall comes in at a sharp angle to connect the two, no one ever swats the fly but, instead, runs the wand against the back wall. The point of the procedure is to illustrate that even though we know "intellectually" that the room is distorted in the way it is, this knowledge does not correct the action, since the action is based on the way we perceive the room and the way we have learned to act with respect to such a perception. After three trials in which he missed the fly, the President, after initial spontaneous laughter, became somewhat irritated, put the wand down and said, "Well, doctor, after all I'm not left-handed."

I presented one or two other demonstrations and we discussed their relationship to programs and messages meant to influence people abroad. Eisenhower got all the points quickly. He related that years ago he had almost given up trying to figure out how the other fellow felt. When he was a young officer in Asia, he said, there was a court-martial case in which a man was being tried for cruelty to a woman to whom he was engaged and with whom he was living. One night the man had told the woman he no longer loved her and threw her out of the house. He was acquitted. The President said he had been shocked at this Oriental conception of justice and remarked to himself at the time: "Boy, but you're a whale of a long way from Abilene, Kansas."

This occasion, to my knowledge, marks the first time a psychologist, in his professional role, had directly drawn a President's attention to the possible value of psychological theory in Government policy-making.

As everyone knows who has worked with these demonstrations in perception, they reveal a great deal about the person to whom they are presented. I have shown them to hundreds of people and always been rewarded by learning more about the person I am with. For example, on two occasions when I have shown the demonstrations to certain well-known persons, each one became so angry with me on failing to "swat the fly" that he picked up his hat and left without even saying goodbye. This rather infantile display of temper occurred presumably because they thought I was trying to show them up.

On the other hand, people of great security and maturity react with an almost childish glee when they are fooled time after time. John Dewey was one of these. I showed him the demonstrations when he was nearly ninety years old. He shuffled around the room clapping his hands and repeating "This is splendid. It demonstrates so clearly what I have always believed."

Another such case was Albert Einstein, a Princeton neighbor, who had a great belly laugh over each demonstration, then leaned back and said, "But this is beautiful." Incidentally, Einstein understood the whole theory behind the "revolving trapezoid window" more quickly than anyone I ever met. The very first time the window oscillated for

Einstein, he had his belly laugh and then said, "Ah ha, you have something there what is not a rectangle."

There is one incident I wish I had been able to record with a camera. One morning, the chairman of the physics department at Princeton telephoned my office to say that Niels Bohr, the Danish physicist, and his wife would like to see our demonstration center at the Princeton psychological laboratories. No sooner had I hung up the phone than a call came from the biology department saying Konrad Lorenz, the Austrian naturalist, would like to come right down to see the demonstrations. Within fifteen minutes Bohr and Lorenz were at the demonstration center. Both were big, powerful men and both talked almost incessantly. At that time we had a full-sized distorted room in which we displayed various illusory phenomena. The floor of the room sloped at a steep angle to the left, since the left wall was twice as high as the right wall. Lorenz and Bohr each took a quick look at the room through a peephole in the door. The sight of people changing size as they walked along the back wall from one corner to another so excited the two men that they flung open the door and walked in. Bohr was the first to enter, with Lorenz close on his heels. Bohr fell immediately and slid clear down to the left-hand corner. Then Lorenz fell and slid down on top of Bohr. Both men, laughing, had to be pulled out of the tangle they were in.

4

My Initiation in Survey Techniques

One of my earliest articles, written in 1934, had the title, "The Social Psychology of Everyday Life." [5] Along with a review of the adequacy and apparent validity of research and writing in social psychology at the time, it contained a plea that social psychologists devote more attention to ongoing problems and devise new techniques for studying them rather than adapt their problems to fit standardized methods. Very often their accountings were partial and temporary because of the host of variables left out of the formulation of the problem.

When I read in 1935 about the surveys being launched and reported in the newspapers by George Gallup, and saw the *Fortune* surveys begun by Elmo Roper and his associates and by Archibald Crossley, I felt that here was a new instrument the social scientist, particularly the social psychologist, had better look into. The survey technique seemed to hold potentialities for the study of genuine problems, for learning how people look at things, and for understanding better than we did why people of various backgrounds, interests, loyalties, and information levels hold the opinions they do.

Because much of the research reported here utilized surveys of opinion, it is relevant to the story to give a brief account of some of my early efforts in the field that led directly into policy research itself. While the survey technique in all its forms is now relatively old hat and part and parcel of the information kit of social scientists, of government at all levels, of aspiring politicians, and, of course, of the market researchers, in the late 1930's there were practically no social scientists who gave any serious consideration to these methods. Most of my social science colleagues at the time either were ignorant about them or tended to belittle them because none of the men doing the pioneer work in the field were members of the academic fraternity.

I therefore welcomed a request from Lester Markel, then Sunday Editor of the *New York Times,* asking if I would look into the newfangled method of "scientific" opinion polling and write some articles about it for the Magazine and News of the Week sections of the *Times,* in connection with the election campaign of 1936.

In preparation for the articles, I went to Princeton to see George Gallup. It was just before the 1936 election; he was predicting the error the *Literary Digest* poll would make as well as reporting his own estimate of the election's outcome. I found him, quite understandably, a rather nervous and anxious man at the time.[6] He gave me a most cordial welcome, was delighted to have a social scientist take his work seriously, and offered his facilities at cost for any research I might want to do. The opportunity to utilize Gallup's facilities was not an insignificant element in my decision in 1936 to accept an offer to join the faculty at Princeton University.

In 1940, I applied to the Rockefeller Foundation for funds to establish an Office of Public Opinion Research at Princeton. The Foundation was generous in responding to the application and renewed its grant for a number of years. The initial purposes of the Office were, at the time, fourfold: (1)

to learn and study public opinion techniques systematically; (2) to gain insights into the psychological aspects of public opinion, how and why it changes, what motivates large segments of the public; (3) to build up an archive of public opinion data for the use of qualified scholars; [7] and (4) to begin to follow the course of American public opinion during the war that had already started in Europe, in which I felt the United States would soon be involved. The Office was first set up in attic space found in the Palmer physics building at Princeton University.

The research on techniques and psychological problems was published in numerous articles, chiefly during the early years of the *Public Opinion Quarterly,* of which I was a founding associate editor, with Harwood Childs as Editor. My research colleagues and I also published a book that put together various studies and was entitled *Gauging Public Opinion.*[8]

Most relevant to the story of policy research are the efforts begun in 1940 by the Office of Public Opinion Research to utilize and adapt survey methods as the European war progressed and the United States became increasingly involved. This research dealt with three kinds of problems: (1) devising questions that would help us to understand more clearly what the American people felt the United States should do vis-à-vis the war in Europe and what differences of opinion there were in various population groups; (2) formulating "trend" questions that could be repeated, either at regular intervals or as events dictated; and (3) testing the reliability of small samples. During 1940 and 1941, the Office of Public Opinion Research obtained all data through the American Institute of Public Opinion at cost; thereafter I set up my own survey facilities, as described later in Chapter 6.

For the benefit of those not familiar with "scientific" sampling of public opinion, it may be useful to describe the procedure briefly. Scientific sampling has been used well over a century in various ways, since it was found by investigators in agriculture, medicine, and industry that a few well-chosen observations could reveal with considerable reliability what the composition of a whole group of items might be. The use of the sampling technique for purposes of gauging public opinion was developed in the mid-1930's. The aim of such sampling is to obtain with relatively few cases a true cross-section of what the statistician calls the "universe" in which he is interested. In most public opinion research, the "universe" is the total adult population, but it can be limited, of course, to any segment of the population, such as youth, men or women only, members of labor unions, or whatever group one wants to study. The fundamental principle is to draw a sample in such a way that everyone in the "universe" in which one is interested has an equal chance of being interviewed. In the 1930's the method used to select a sample was to try to select respondents with reference to certain controlled quotas that were known from other data. For example, in obtaining a sample of the adult population of the United States, the proper proportion of people was selected according to the geographical sections of the country within which they lived. Then within each section further categories were made depending on the degree of urbanization. Interviewers were chosen who could question people in the specified areas. Each interviewer was given an assignment which instructed him to select a specified number of people representing different economic status groups, a specified number of Negroes, a specified number of farmers, etc. The interviewer was further told how many men and how many women to interview and was asked to distribute his interviewing among persons of different age groups. Because this method left so much of the decision of whom to interview up to the interviewer himself and since even the most conscientious interviewer might introduce conscious or unconscious bias in his selection, a more reliable method for obtaining a random or "probability" sample was devised in the mid-1940's and is the method generally used today in all parts of the world where sufficient data are available to give an accurate picture of the "universe" of people from whom the sample is to be drawn. A short description of modern probability sampling will be found in Note 9, pp. 167 to 169.

If proper sampling methods are used, it is possible to obtain quite precise representations of the opinion of a whole nation's population with surprisingly few cases. The margin of error in a sample of, say, 3,000 cases is around 4 per cent; the margin of error in 1,000 cases is only around 6 per cent.

Many of the studies reported here utilized extremely small samples of only 100, 200, or 300 cases. I devised and tested this method of utilizing small samples in 1940 because of two practical motives in addition to the intrinsic theoretical interest the subject had. I felt that if the United States became involved in the war and we had established the reliability of small samples, there would be the possibility of obtaining information on the reactions of the American people with maximum speed and minimum cost. Second, I foresaw the potentiality of utilizing the survey technique clandestinely in enemy or neutral territory to get information that might in one way or another help the war effort. The small samples set up by the Office of Public Opinion Research were designed by Frederick Mosteller, then a graduate student at Princeton and on our office staff, and later Chairman of Harvard's Department of Mathematical Statistics. The results of these early studies on small samples [10] have since been confirmed by many other people in a wide variety of situations. We predicted gubernatorial state elections, primary elections, and plebiscites. The results obtained from our tiny samples of 100, 200, or 300 cases seldom differed from the final returns by more than 6 per cent. All small samples were at that time designed on the quota system with the proper number of people interviewed in different sections of the country, in cities or towns of different sizes, among people of various economic groups, and properly proportioned by sex and age.

In one of the studies, I deliberately tried to simulate the conditions under which one might have to make a survey in enemy territory in predicting a plebiscite on conscription held in Canada. Here we used only 200 cases. Interviewing was begun one week before the plebiscite. Only two interviewers were employed, neither of whom had had any experience in public opinion polling. One of them, fluent in French, was sent to the Province of Quebec, the other to Ontario. The interviewers had to memorize the questions, ask them in casual conversations, make no written notes during the interview, but record the answers as soon as possible after they had left the respondent. The two interviewers were given only very general ideas as to the method of obtaining a sample, differentiating their interviewees properly between those of rural and those of urban areas and classifying them by occupation. Above all, the interviewers were told to keep moving. Results were telegraphed to us before the plebiscite actually occurred. The difference between the vote as predicted in our small sample and the final plebiscite was 4.5 per cent.

The questions asked on surveys are designed by the investigator. In many of the studies reported here, I had the benefit of consultation with various aides of President Roosevelt or with other persons familiar with the problems and issues to be studied. All questions are carefully pre-tested on a number of people to make sure the questions contain no bias and that they are readily understandable. Questions are revised until they are found to be easily comprehensible to a sample of the wide range of persons of whom they will be asked. The interviewers who ask the questions have been carefully trained by the organization employing them and are instructed to make insofar as possible verbatim reports of all replies which are not answered in a simple Yes-No, Agree-Disagree fashion. There is now a huge technical literature in the survey field reporting numerous studies concerned with the selection and training of interviewers as well as with the wording of questions.

My first attempt to utilize surveys for policy research began in September 1940, when Nelson Rockefeller, then Coordinator of Inter-American Affairs for President Roosevelt, asked me to set up mechanisms which would gauge public opinion in Latin America. Roosevelt was eager to know what effect, if any, Nazi propaganda was having on the opinions of people in that part of the world. George Gallup and I set up a nonprofit research corporation, American Social Surveys, with funds from the United States Office of Emergency Management, for the operation contemplated.[11] In the course of this work, Lloyd Free managed the first public opinion survey ever done in Brazil, which we had chosen for a pilot study. Leonard Doob, professor of psychology at Yale, worked with us in analyzing the propaganda coming into Latin America, and we trained men to assume posts in several Latin American countries and to carry out research assignments for us.

Since all the studies were done with Government funds, they were classified and I am unable to report any of the results obtained. But I am mentioning this early undertaking because it opened the door to the public opinion research done for Roosevelt. Briefly, the story goes as follows. Early in December 1940, I was asked by Nelson Rockefeller to see Mr. James W. Young, then Undersecretary of Commerce and a man who had demonstrated great skill in breaking German morale during World War I; he had been formerly president of the J. Walter Thompson advertising company. Jim was in charge of the communications division of Nelson's office. The two of us for awhile had adjoining offices in one of the old brownstone Rockefeller family buildings at 11 West Fifty-fourth Street in New York. Jim was a shy, wise, and most lovable man, full of a sort of Will Rogers humor. I remember one evening when we were having dinner together he commented that "the only difference between an advertising man and a professor is a sense of direction." One of the most cherished books in my library is its tiniest volume, containing a lecture Jim had given at the University of Chicago with the bold title, *How to Create an Idea.*

Jim became interested in the research I was doing on American opinion, the types of questions being asked and the trends I was establishing, and thought the President should know about them. I prepared some reports especially for him, which he passed on to Mrs. Anna Rosenberg, a close associate of Roosevelt's during that time. This was the beginning of my work with the President.

Before continuing that story, I shall report a few of the activities that went on simultaneously with the research on public opinion and the attempt to set up a program on Latin America for the office of the Coordinator of Inter-American Affairs.

5

An Idea that Mushroomed

In London during February of 1938, Professor John B. Whitton of Princeton's Department of Political Science had a conversation with Edward R. Murrow, which led to a pioneering research undertaking. Murrow was then director of radio talks for the Columbia Broadcasting System in New York and was impressed with the astute use being made of radio propaganda by the Nazi propaganda minister, Joseph Goebbels. Murrow and Whitton agreed that it was high time a systematic analysis be made of Axis radio propaganda.

To give the idea a preliminary trial, Whitton engaged Mr. Thomas Grandin, set up a listening post in a Montmartre hotel, and began monitoring Axis radio broadcasts. In 1939 the Geneva Research Center, which Whitton directed, published Grandin's little book, *The Political Use of the Radio*. When Whitton returned to Princeton, a small committee, including Professor Harwood Childs and myself, was set up to work out plans for a continuing study of shortwave propaganda.

By November of 1939, a grant of $20,000 was obtained from the Rockefeller Foundation, thanks largely to the interest and help of Mr. John Marshall. Mr. Harold Graves,

Jr., was engaged to head the research. The Princeton Listening Center was set up in an old house on Alexander Street, loaned for the purpose by the Institute for Advanced Study in Princeton. Graves recruited a small and able staff of technicians, interpreters, and analysts, and began to turn out biweekly reports of shortwave broadcasts from Berlin, London, Rome, Paris, and Moscow. My own role in the operation was to assist in devising various methods of content-analysis of the vast material obtained in order to understand better the psychology behind Nazi propaganda and possibly help predict Axis moves.

By April of 1941, the Center had published twenty biweekly reports digesting and analyzing shortwave broadcasts from England, Germany, France, and Italy, and had compiled ninety typescript volumes containing approximately fifteen million words. All of the Center's material has been filed in Princeton University's Firestone Library.[12]

One of the arts developed by Harold Graves and his associates was that of predicting German military operations from the content of German propaganda. For example, in June of 1940, I asked Harold what he thought about the possibility of a German invasion of Britain in the near future. After reviewing German propaganda of the last week or two, Harold reported that all signs pointed to a massive air assault on England within the next three weeks but did not indicate an assault by sea or land. The continuous heavy air attacks on England began, as predicted, in July. Harold made the prediction concerning both the assault and its timing on the basis of his experience as to how long a period usually elapsed between a German propaganda build-up and military action.

The value of the Center's reports soon became apparent to a number of Government departments and agencies. John Marshall of the Rockefeller Foundation urged the State Department to establish a monitoring service on a national scale, patterned after the Princeton pilot project. Mr. Breckenridge Long, then Assistant Secretary of State, wrote Mr. James Lawrence Fly, Chairman of the Federal Communications Commission, urging that the FCC undertake the job. And Chairman Fly, a man of courage and vision, started the ball rolling.

In early March of 1941, Mr. Fly asked me to head up a national foreign broadcast monitoring service, for which he had funds and which he wanted to organize as quickly as possible. I told Fly the responsibilities I had to the public opinion research I was doing under foundation auspices at Princeton as well as the obligation I had to carry on with Nelson Rockefeller and the research on public opinion in Latin America. And there were also University commitments. I suggested Lloyd Free's name to Mr. Fly as the person for the job.

Lloyd talked to Mr. Fly as soon as he returned from Brazil, where he had been doing the survey for the Coordinator of Inter-American Affairs. Lloyd was interested in the challenge the position presented both in its organizational and research aspects, and accepted the office of Director. Lloyd obtained the services of Harold Graves as Assistant to the Director. (Graves at the time was only twenty-six years old; hence Civil Service approval to give him the title of Assistant Director could not be obtained!) The Princeton Listening Center was of course disbanded and many of its staff moved with Graves to the new operation.

I shall never forget my first visit to the large old warehouse in Washington that had been transformed into the headquarters for the Foreign Broadcast Monitoring Service (FBMS). I was with Free and Graves, the only two men then definitely signed up to help give life to a building that had dozens and dozens of empty offices, that needed to be filled quickly with equipment and, above all, with trained personnel for the various jobs of monitoring, translating, analyzing, and reporting—and all of this on a twenty-four-hour, seven-day-a-week basis.

The FBMS had various functions. One was to collect and to disseminate news, a most important service at a time when correspondents were being increasingly barred from various parts of the world because of the war. A long daily account of all monitored propaganda, the equivalent of a daily newspaper, was published by FBMS, and two ticker tapes provided news services to key agencies of the Government. Another function was to provide special reports analyzing propaganda. A third function was to collect and disseminate intelligence, as well as to predict Axis moves, both military and political.

For example, FBMS was always able to tell when the Axis was going to launch an offensive in North Africa. When things were quiet, the Italian units were left up front and the German units brought back for rest. During such a period, the number of references to Italian units in Axis broadcasts always greatly outnumbered the references to German units. But as soon as the German units got back to the line, a tip-off to an offensive, the proportion of references to German units would increase. The prediction of Axis moves was made possible because the Germans used propaganda as a strategic and tactical arm; hence their propagandists knew ahead of time what was coming and set about preparing for it. On the other hand, any German organization comparable to the FBMS would have been quite baffled, for the simple reason that United States propagandists never knew what was going to happen on the military front.

By the spring of 1942 there were approximately five hundred people employed, with an annual budget of two million dollars. Monitoring stations had been established near Washington, D.C., in Portland, Oregon, in San Francisco, in Texas, and in Puerto Rico; an office had also been set up in liaison with the British Broadcasting Corporation in London.

A paragraph from a letter written to Professor Whitton by Harold Graves, Jr., on February 20, 1942, reveals the significant mushrooming that had occurred since the first days of the Princeton Listening Center:

> You would be interested to see how gigantic the Princeton idea has grown to be. We are receiving now, I should guess, around 500,000 words a day in 15 languages from 25 transmitters. We furnish one wire service of 20,000 words a day to 13 Government departments, agencies, and major units of departments and agencies, and another wire service of 60,000 words a day to the Coordinator of Information, a published daily report of 80,000 words to 225 officials and an analysis of the week, amounting to 20,000 words to 250 different people.

The monitoring and analysis of shortwave broadcasts has now become a regular part of the Government's intelligence service. The agency which handles them is known as the Foreign Broadcast Intelligence Service.

6

Our Work Interests FDR

I have already mentioned that an unexpected upshot of the research done in Nelson Rockefeller's office when he served as Coordinator of Inter-American Affairs was that it led to an expression of interest by President Roosevelt in some of the research done by the Office of Public Opinion Research on the reaction of the American people to the war in Europe.

In the spring of 1940, Mrs. Anna Rosenberg first told me that she was certain the President would like to see some of my public opinion material. I therefore carefully chose a few of the questions we had asked through the facilities of the American Institute of Public Opinion and gave them to her. She showed them to the President within a week, said he was definitely interested in them and would like more. One of the questions that particularly intrigued him was: "Which of these two things do you think is more important for the United States to try to do, to keep out of war ourselves or to help England win, even at the risk of getting into the war?" The results as of July 1940 showed that 59 per cent thought we should keep out of the war and 37 per cent were willing to risk war to help England. Since Roosevelt said he would appreciate it if this question could be asked periodically, it became one of the questions frequently used, as reported in the discussion of "trend" questions in the next chapter.

I was also told that the President would like any material available on public reaction to certain steps this country might take to help England. Clearly, he was already beginning to think about the possibility of some lend-lease arrangement to modify the Neutrality Law that then tied his hands. Accordingly, further questions were asked through the Gallup Poll mechanism.

In August of 1940, about seven months before the Lend-Lease Act was passed by Congress, I transmitted data concerning the shipment of food and war materials to England in order to prevent her defeat by Germany. At that time 80 per cent favored such a policy. But when people were asked if the Neutrality Law should be changed so England could borrow money from our Government to buy more food and war materials in the United States, only 43 per cent were in favor and 47 per cent disapproved. At this time the President was most particularly concerned with American opinion as to whether the Neutrality Law should be changed to permit American ships to carry war supplies to England. The pattern of a continuing trend was already quite apparent: in July of 1940, 54 per cent answered "No," but by August the figure had dropped to 47 per cent.

Data sent the President in February 1941 on the lend-lease problem further revealed the state of mind of the American people on the issue of whether or not the United States should lend war materials to the British to be paid back in the same materials or other goods after the war was over. On this issue, 65 per cent expressed approval; only 20 per cent were opposed, the rest giving qualified answers or having no opinion. Of the 63 per cent of the public who indicated in February 1941 that they had been following the discussion of the President's lend-lease bill in Congress, 58 per cent thought the bill should be passed, only 21 per cent were opposed, with the rest having no clear-cut opinions.

Two other examples of reports sent the President during pre-Pearl Harbor days illustrate what interested him. The bearing of them on his overall policy planning is clear.

In May of 1941 we asked a sample of the American people if they thought President Roosevelt had gone too far in helping Britain, or not far enough? The replies at that time were: too far, 19 per cent; about right, 54 per cent; not far enough, 18 per cent; and no opinion, 9 per cent. This was another of the questions the President said he would like to have repeated from time to time, and the subsequent results are shown in the next chapter.

Immediately after Germany invaded the Soviet Union on June 22, 1941, we asked two questions, each deliberately slanted in a different direction and included on the "split-ballot" used by the American Institute of Public Opinion. The split-ballot was a device for soliciting answers to questions asked in different ways at the same time from entirely comparable populations. The first slanted question was: "Some people say that since Germany is now fighting Russia, as well as Britain, it is not as necessary for this country to help Britain. Do you agree or disagree with this?" Seventy-three per cent of the American people disagreed with the proposition. The other question, slanted a different way, was: "Some people say that, since Germany will probably defeat Russia within a few weeks and then turn her full strength against Britain, it is more important than ever that we help Britain. Do you agree or disagree with this?" Seventy-one per cent agreed.

So it was quite clear that opinion was what might be described as "solid"; people were not easily amenable to the suggestions they contained. Both questions revealed practically identical majorities in the same direction. Furthermore, analysis of replies in terms of the religious and economic backgrounds of respondents showed no appreciable differences of opinion. Mrs. Rosenberg telephoned on July 18 to say that the President was particularly relieved to learn of the uniformity of opinion within the population.

More and more requests came from the White House as American involvement in the war increased and particularly, of course, after the Japanese attacked the United States at Pearl Harbor on December 7, 1941. Since the Office of Public Opinion Research was entirely supported by foundation funds, and since I wanted to remain a free agent and not become involved in any of the new organizations being discussed in Washington at the time, I was baffled as to how information relating to policy and procedures of the type we had gathered in the course of our research could be financed. But Fortune intervened.

Shortly after Pearl Harbor, a Princeton neighbor whom I had not met, Mr. Gerard B. Lambert, called one Sunday morning to ask if he could drive out to see me about the work I was doing for the President. He had just heard about this from our mutual friend, Winfield Riefler, then with the Institute for Advanced Study. We talked all morning and continued the discussion at dinner at his house that evening.

Lambert's remarkable and varied career is reported in his autobiography, *All Out of Step*,[13] published shortly after his seventieth birthday. He was one of the country's greatest advertising men, who had very early used survey techniques in research; he was a financial genius, yachtsman, painter, musician and, at the present writing, is one of the few people in the country who does Double-crostic puzzles in his head without the aid of a pencil. Lambert had retired in his early thirties. Now he wondered if there was any way he could help in the work for the President by way of contributing ideas, writing reports, or financing.

Up to this time I had been using the facilities of the American Institute of Public Opinion at cost price to obtain data for much of our research and for all questions dealing with reactions to the war. Lambert suggested we set up our own nationwide survey mechanism, comparable to Gallup's, so we would be free to launch studies at any time they were required; he would gladly cover all expenses. We told Harold Dodds, then President of Princeton University, what our plans were and he gave us his blessing.

So, early in 1942 we created a nonprofit corporation, The Research Council, Inc., and began the task of designing our sample and hiring interviewers. On the first of these jobs, we had the able assistance of Frederick Mosteller, who designed all the samples set up by the Office of Public Opinion Research. Dr. Seldon Menefee was engaged to travel all over the country to select interviewers, who were then trained by him and by others sent out from the Princeton office. The headquarters of the Research Council were identical with those of the Office of Public Opinion Research. Incidentally, all tabulating equipment in the Office of Public Opinion Research had been loaned to us by the International Business Machines Corporation.

In a few months' time we were in business, using nationwide samples of 1,200 cases which Fred had selected as the most efficient for our purposes. In addition, we carefully designed small nationwide samples of 300 cases and found interviewers willing to drop, on call, anything they were doing in order to fulfill our small-sample quota of interviews. The reliability of this latter device of utilizing small samples had been tested, as already reported, and Lambert and I thought we might often during the war have need to obtain quick and rough indices of public reaction. In order

to keep a constant check on the reliability of these small
sample operations, we always repeated in our next regular
survey of 1,200 cases any question on which we had used
the small sample. Results never varied by more than 6 per
cent.

At the end of each month, I sent Lambert's New York
office a report of the amount of money spent during the
month, and a check was returned to the Research Council
immediately. There was no special limit placed on our expenses: we undertook any research Jerry and I thought
would be helpful or any that was requested by the White
House.

The Lamberts' large, fully staffed house at 78 Kalorama
Circle in Washington became my second home for most of
the war years. Here Jerry and I could, without interruption,
plan our research and prepare our reports; here we held
conferences and entertained many of the President's associates with whom we worked, as well as other officials. We
deliberately made a point of being seen as little as possible
in Government offices or agencies in order to minimize
curiosity and preserve the informality of our relationships.

As our work with the White House increased, Mrs. Rosenberg felt there should be more direct liaison with the President through someone who was regularly in Washington. She
therefore introduced us to one of the President's six "anonymous assistants," David K. Niles, who quickly saw the potential value of what we were trying to do and got everything
to the President without change or editing. Certain reports
dealing with labor or economic problems went to Dr. Isador
Lubin, another of the six "anonymous assistants" in the
White House. A few of the reports dealing with ideas for
speeches the President might make went to Samuel Rosenman, whose office in the White House was very close to the
President's. The President told us to bring directly to his

personal secretary, Miss Grace Tully, anything we thought particularly important for him to see. It was through Miss Tully that I kept the President's "trend" charts up to date.

A word should be said about the preparation of reports for the President. A great deal of valuable material social scientists uncover or create is presented in so academic or slipshod a fashion that no busy person is going to waste time digging out what may be of significance. Jerry and I spent many hours discussing any report we planned to hand in, made many revisions, always eliminating anything that was not completely relevant to the major point. All reports were kept as brief as possible; most were no more than two or three pages. We always tried to remember that the President was one of the busiest men in the world and would completely lose interest if we became verbose or technical. We marked on the margin with red pencil especially crucial data or conclusions, and I sometimes drew a face on the margin beside data that brought good or bad news. All reports were carefully typed. Nothing was allowed to formalize them. Wherever possible, results were put in simple bar graph or chart form. Major results and conclusions were always given first, the necessary details later. The informality of our relationship with the President is reflected in an amusing exchange of letters he had with Lambert as reported in Note 14, pp. 171f.

Since the use of and reliance on public opinion surveys has now become standard practice for American presidents, it may be interesting to know what use FDR, whose tenure in office overlapped the initial development of the survey technique in the mid-1930's, made of survey data.

Roosevelt regarded the reports sent him the way a general would regard information turned in by his intelligence services as he planned the strategy of a campaign. As far as I am aware, Roosevelt never altered his goals because public opinion appeared against him or was uninformed. Rather he utilized such information to try to bring the public around more quickly or more effectively to the course of action he felt was best for the country. I am certain he would have agreed with Churchill's comment that "Nothing is more dangerous than to live in the temperamental atmosphere of a Gallup poll, always taking one's pulse and taking one's temperature . . . There is only one duty, only one safe course, and that is to try to be right and not to fear to do or say what you believe to be right."

Finally, I want to emphasize that no claim is made here that the data and suggestions Lambert and I provided the President were crucial in his decisions. But actions taken were certainly very often completely consistent with our recommendations.

7

American Reactions during World War II

Of all our material sent President Roosevelt during World War II, nothing interested him more than the trend charts, which repeated the same questions from time to time to reflect the movement of opinion as circumstances changed. When the first copies were transmitted to the President, I had them carefully drawn and deliberately left considerable space on the right of the charts so they could continue to be filled in periodically. They were put in a hard binding to give them an identity of their own amidst all other papers received. As new points came in, I extended the lines myself in Miss Tully's office.[15]

It was, of course, exceedingly difficult to know what questions would be worth repeating, since a question that made sense at one time might make no sense somewhat later. An example of one question that was thought of just in the nick of time is whether the American people thought the Allies were winning or losing the war. The shift in popular opinion is shown by the dotted line on Chart IV.

The charts were confidential. They were kept up to date by a few other officials in Washington to whom the data were given, and several times ambassadors from friendly powers flew up to Princeton to look at my master charts, since I did not want to let them have copies of their own.

The excitement of following the trends of opinion, learning how they were affected by events, and wondering where they would go next is difficult for anyone to recapture at this distance in time, now that the outcome is a part of history. Perhaps the drama of the situation can be in part recaptured by looking at Chart I, which gives the trends of opinion up to the time of the mass air raids on Britain, clearly a low point in American morale, and then by turning to Chart II, which shows how the American people were lifted to fresh optimism and new determination to help England, even at the risk of war, by the successful outcome of the Battle of Britain, when, in Churchill's famous sentence, "Never in the field of human conflict was so much owed by so many to so few." [16]

Chart III shows other trends prior to Pearl Harbor. Charts IV and V indicate some of the trends of American opinion from Pearl Harbor to the German capitulation.

The trend shown in Chart VI indicates the uncanny way in which the President was able to balance public opinion around his policies. The precise question asked was, as already mentioned, one of those the President said he hoped could be repeated at frequent intervals: "So far as you personally are concerned, do you think President Roosevelt has gone too far in his policies of helping Britain, or not far enough?" In spite of the fact that United States aid to Britain constantly increased after May of 1941, the proportion of people who thought the President had gone too far, about right, or not far enough remained fairly constant. This was precisely the situation he wanted to maintain during these critical months; hence his eagerness to learn the results of our periodic soundings.

Since there was considerable discussion about the pos-

Chart I.

Some trends of opinion up to Battle of Britain

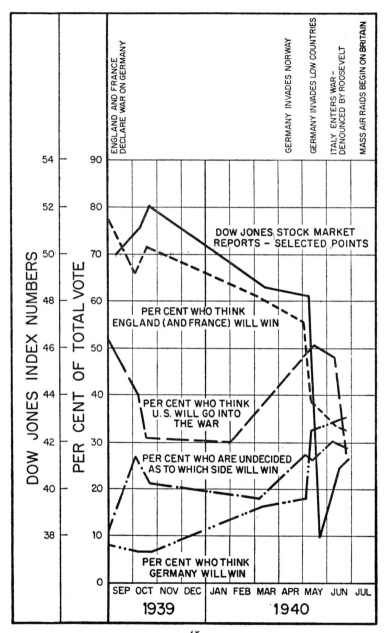

Chart II.

Some trends of opinion prior to Pearl Harbor

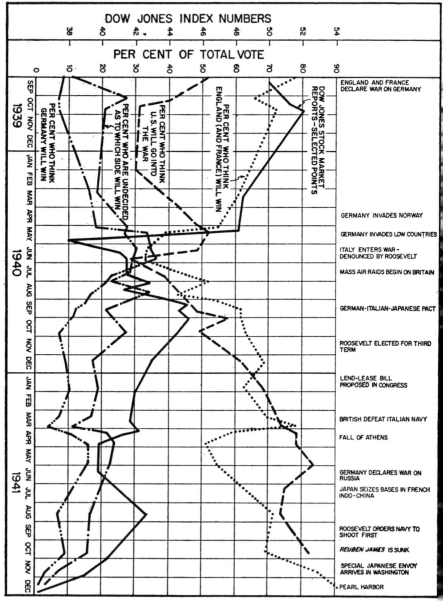

46

Chart III.

Further trends of opinion prior to Pearl Harbor

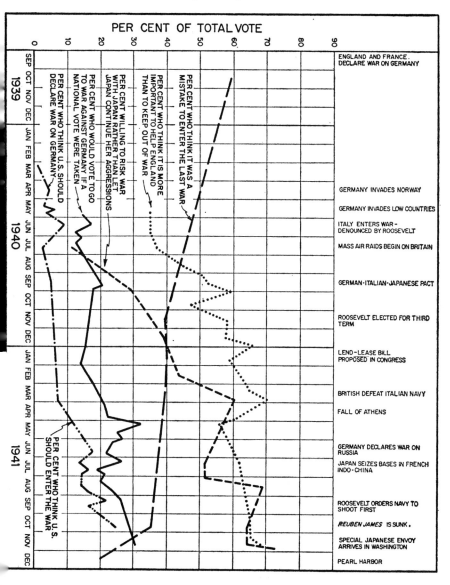

Chart IV.

Some trends of opinion after United States entry into war

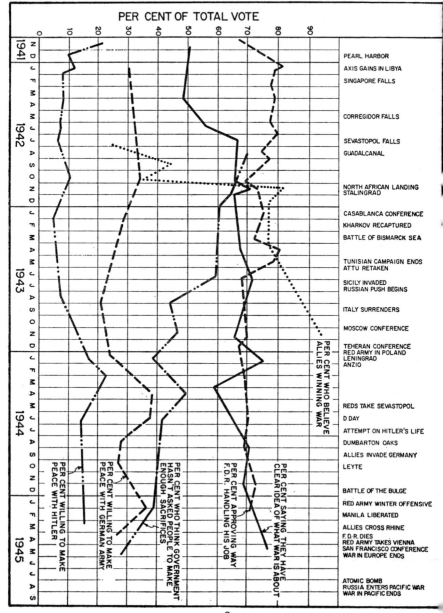

PER CENT OF TOTAL VOTE

1941
N
D — PEARL HARBOR

1942
J — AXIS GAINS IN LIBYA
F — SINGAPORE FALLS
M
A
M — CORREGIDOR FALLS
J
J — SEVASTOPOL FALLS
A — GUADALCANAL
S
O
N — NORTH AFRICAN LANDING / STALINGRAD
D

1943
J — CASABLANCA CONFERENCE
F — KHARKOV RECAPTURED
M — BATTLE OF BISMARCK SEA
A
M — TUNISIAN CAMPAIGN ENDS / ATTU RETAKEN
J
J — SICILY INVADED / RUSSIAN PUSH BEGINS
A
S — ITALY SURRENDERS
O — MOSCOW CONFERENCE
N
D — TEHERAN CONFERENCE / RED ARMY IN POLAND / LENINGRAD / ANZIO

1944
J
F
M
A
M — REDS TAKE SEVASTOPOL
J — D DAY
J — ATTEMPT ON HITLER'S LIFE
A — DUMBARTON OAKS
S — ALLIES INVADE GERMANY
O — LEYTE
N
D — BATTLE OF THE BULGE

1945
J — RED ARMY WINTER OFFENSIVE
F — MANILA LIBERATED
M — ALLIES CROSS RHINE
A — F.D.R. DIES / RED ARMY TAKES VIENNA / SAN FRANCISCO CONFERENCE / WAR IN EUROPE ENDS
M
J
J — ATOMIC BOMB / RUSSIA ENTERS PACIFIC WAR / WAR IN PACIFIC ENDS
A
S

PER CENT WHO BELIEVE ALLIES WINNING WAR

PER CENT WILLING TO MAKE PEACE WITH HITLER

PER CENT WILLING TO MAKE PEACE WITH GERMAN ARMY

PER CENT WHO THINK GOVERNMENT HASN'T ASKED PEOPLE TO MAKE ENOUGH SACRIFICES

PER CENT APPROVING WAY F.D.R. HANDLING HIS JOB

PER CENT SAYING THEY HAVE CLEAR IDEA OF WHAT WAR IS ABOUT

48

Chart V.

Further trends of opinion after United States entry into war

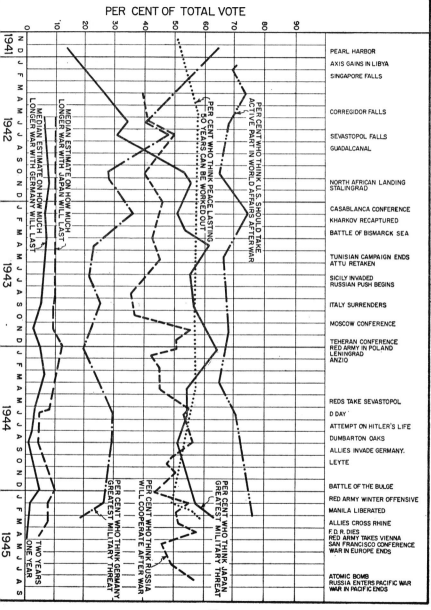

PER CENT OF TOTAL VOTE

49

Chart VI.

Opinion on Roosevelt's aid-to-Britain policies

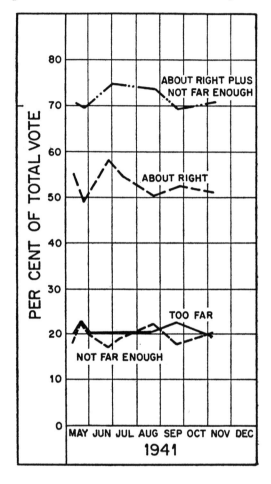

sibility of a German peace offensive and hope after Pearl Harbor that the German general staff might itself be willing to negotiate an acceptable peace, Roosevelt carefully followed the two trends differentiating the extent of the willingness of Americans to make peace with the German Army, on the one hand, and Hitler on the other hand (Chart IV).

The high majority which consistently felt the United States should take an active part in world affairs when the war was over (Chart V) clearly demonstrated that some of the individuals, groups, and newspapers urging an isolationist stand were speaking only for a tiny minority.

And of course the President kept his eye on the trend of the answers to the question frequently asked by the American Institute of Public Opinion as well as by our own office as to whether or not people approved the way he was handling his whole job (Chart IV).

8

Public Views on the War's Progress

It was of course imperative that the American people never become overly sanguine or self-confident about the war's progress. From time to time, in addition to the trend surveys, we made special studies to help guide the President and other civilian war leaders in bracing people for the long, hard road ahead and for occasional setbacks.

One of these checks on public opinion was especially concerned with the American reaction to the war in Italy during the spring of 1944. At that time, some seven months after the initial landing on the Italian mainland on September 4, 1943, and the surrender of Italy on September 8, 1943, the German army was still putting up bitter and skillful resistance. It was not until the spring of 1945 that Italy was cleared of German troops.

In order to compare public reaction to the Italian campaign with the reaction to two other phases of the war, the Allied bombing of Germany and the war in the Pacific, during the second week of April 1944 we asked a nationwide sample of Americans if they thought the fighting on the Italian front was going as well as they expected or slower than they expected. Only 28 per cent felt it was going as well as expected and 60 per cent said slower. As to the war in the Pacific, 80 per cent felt it was going as well as expected. And when we asked if people had the impression that the Allied bombing of Germany was increasing or decreasing the fighting spirit of the German people, nearly half (48 per cent) felt it was decreasing the fighting spirit of Germans and only 25 per cent thought it was increasing this spirit. The rest of the people asked either felt it was making no difference or they had no opinion.

These results were transmitted to the President and to Secretary of War Henry L. Stimson on April 19, 1944, with the suggestion that understatement be used in discussing operations.

On May 18, Secretary Stimson held a news conference, which the *New York Times* reported under the headline, STIMSON PREDICTS HARD ROAD IN ITALY.[17] In this conference, Stimson anticipated unusually heavy fighting ahead when the Allies hit the so-called "Hitler Line" still in front of them in Italy. "The Germans still do not attach Hitler's name lightly to any fortification," said Stimson; and "It is to be expected that the enemy defense there and the reinforcements which may come from reserves will render the next step in the Allied campaign exceedingly difficult. We do not wish to make claims in advance nor to magnify our gains."

Likewise, in the President's radio talk to the American people on June 5, 1944, in which, among other things, he discussed the capture of Rome the previous day, he took the occasion to point out that "Victory still lies some distance ahead. . . . It will be tough and it will be costly."

Some three months before the capture of Rome, early on the morning of March 1, 1944, we had received a call from David Niles at the White House. His chief task for the President was to keep in touch with problems and interests of minority groups and advise on policy relevant to them. He said the President was concerned about the effect further bombing of Rome might have on Catholic morale and support of the war effort. Could we find out at once what Catholics thought about this?

Accordingly, Lambert and I decided to utilize our special small sample of 300 cases. It will be remembered that the interviewers involved in this kind of sampling had pledged themselves in advance to drop anything they were doing and to undertake telegraphic surveys.

Lambert and I talked over the way the question should be phrased and telegraphed the question, together with instructions to report results by telephone or telegraph at once, and to include the religious affiliations of respondents. The question to be asked was: If our military leaders believe it will be necessary to bomb Rome but take every precaution to avoid damage to its religious shrines, would you approve or disapprove of this decision?

All replies were in by late afternoon the same day. A hand tabulation was made and the results telephoned to Dave Niles early in the evening. The results showed that an overwhelming majority of Catholics as well as Protestants would approve a decision to bomb Rome if our military leaders thought it essential: among Catholics, 66 per cent approved, 27 per cent disapproved, and 7 per cent had no opinion, while among Protestants the respective figures were 81 per cent, 13 per cent, and 6 per cent.

Rome was heavily bombed two days later, on March 3, the first bombing of Rome since mid-August. The targets successfully damaged were railroad yards and airports, both important at that time for the movement of German troops.[18]

Later surveys on our national sample, done subsequently to the bombing, confirmed the results of this small sample telegraphic survey and were transmitted both to Mr. Niles for the President and to Henry L. Stimson, Secretary of War.

9

Suggestions for Presidential Speeches

From time to time Lambert and I felt it would be helpful if we could demonstrate to the President how the plausibility of his speeches might be improved and how cooperation with Congress or the public could be increased. Sometimes the suggestions dealt with content, sometimes with the tone of a speech. Three of these suggestions follow, each of which was adopted in principle.

In his State of the Union Message to Congress on January 6, 1942, the President had indicated the specific number of planes, tanks, anti-aircraft guns, and tons of shipping that he had set as the production goals for the calendar year and for 1943. Since there was subsequently considerable concern in the press that these goals were not being met and might not be, together with a good deal of confusion about production figures, we thought it wise that in his next State of the Union Message the President should not again exhibit the apparently American characteristic of overstating what we will do. Accordingly, we sent two memoranda to the President on December 15, 1942, "one short and one longer —to suit your convenience." The longer version also included simple bar graphs and charts based on public opinion polls that documented the points made.[19] The shorter version, which follows, consisted of only one page plus charts. We wrote that

Of all methods of building confidence, none is more certain than the habit of performing better than has been promised.

It is recommended that all predictions, quotas, and statements related to war production for 1943 be deliberately based on figures below the minimum which will be achieved. It is a policy of understatement and overperformance. Acceptance of this principle will build new, deeply rooted confidence in the Administration; discourage the enemy by establishing confidence in our statements; handicap enemy propaganda; and remove a point of criticism by opponents and legislative bodies.

Attached are charts derived from recent public opinion surveys pertinent to this subject, and showing: 26 per cent interviewed think the President has not brought production up to promises; examples of dangerously wide swings in public opinion coincident with Rommel's advance and the African campaign; how the public forgets production quotas—hence, new quotas may safely be announced. If understatement policy is adopted, public will be constantly reminded when quotas are periodically exceeded.

The State of the Union Message given on January 7, 1943, made no mention of specific production quotas to be met. Without referring to fixed goals, the President managed to give an encouraging picture of the nation's productive capacity, which he termed a "miracle." A *New York Times* correspondent noted that "large segments of Congress, which long had been disturbed by confusing reports of production progress, were heartened by the President's detailed report." The following suggestion concerning the advisability of using a conciliatory approach to Congress rather than one which in any way could be interpreted as truculent is self-explanatory. The survey upon which the data were based was a spot-check of 300 people along the Eastern seaboard, properly distributed by income, occupation, age, and sex. The report was sent to David Niles on December 21, 1942. It recommended a speech by the President clearly conciliatory in character and striking the keynote of cooperation between the President and the Congress. The supporting data included indicated that the people considered it essential that cooperation should exist between the President and Congress and that it was more necessary for the President to cooperate with the Congress than for Congress to cooperate with the President.[20] In other words, failure on the part of the President to cooperate would be resented more than failure by Congress.

The memorandum was followed the next day by a further note. Again a spot-check of 300 cases was used to get a feeling of public reaction. We stated as a supplementary suggestion to our memorandum the previous day that after referring to the need for Congressional cooperation and the President's desire for it, the President should point out that there are, however, certain decisions which he—as Commander-in-Chief —must make very rapidly in the interest of maximum prosecution of the war. For our survey had shown that 78 per cent of the American people felt that it was quite all right for the President to make some important decisions before consulting Congress if this were essential for the war effort and if consultation with Congress would delay the prosecution of the war.

In reporting on the State of the Union Message of January 7, 1943, which was interrupted by applause forty-five times, W. H. Lawrence said in the *New York Times* that the message "was well received by Representatives and Senators, who thought it was conciliatory in tone." The same issue of that newspaper contained a special article, also on page 1, by C. P. Trussell, with the headline "Message Tone Conciliatory, Members of Congress Feel."

The same suggestion was repeated in a later memorandum to Samuel I. Rosenman, who assisted Roosevelt in preparing his speeches. The memorandum was dated February 25, 1944, and was passed on at that time because of a great deal of criticism that had been recently leveled at Roosevelt for his veto of a tax bill. The documentation for this renewed suggestion that the President try to take a more cooperative approach to Congress and the public was based on questions which pre-tested alternative methods of achieving the same goal: "scolding" vs. "pleading for cooperation." The memorandum of transmittal stated that, in designing the questions, the word "scolding" was deliberately used because it was found through advance testing to be the best way to express many complex characteristics which could not otherwise be clearly defined for respondents.

The exact question asked was as follows: "When the President makes a radio talk he frequently scolds small groups who are not helping fully in the war effort. Do you think the President would get better results by asking people kindly to cooperate or by scolding them?" A majority of 63 per cent opted for "asking kindly" and only 22 per cent favored the "scolding approach." Another question in the same vein asked if people thought the President got better cooperation from the public if, in his radio talks, he appealed to them in a friendly way or made fun of them. Here, 90 per cent favored the "friendly approach," only 8 per cent favored "scolding" or "making fun" of people. In a third question, we asked people to suppose the President decided to give a radio talk on the general subject of rationing. We then presented the same two alternative approaches for people to choose from: scolding those who are not cooperating and appealing for people to cooperate and follow the rules. On this question, 90 per cent favored the "cooperative approach."

Evidence that the President had altered his somewhat impatient tone toward Congress was reflected in his message of March 31, 1944, giving his reasons for allowing the Servicemen's Voting Bill to become law without his signature. In reporting on the message, Mr. Trussell of the *New York Times* of that date wrote: "While members observed that the President had raised anew the constitutional questions which caused bitter deadlocks and resulted in Congressional acceptance of the conditional provisions now criticized, the reception given to today's message was more kindly than that given the one of Jan. 25 in which the President called a prior States' rights' voting measure 'a fraud' on the service men and the American people. This afternoon the 'temperate' and 'cooperative' tone of the new message was commended from the House floor and in the capitol corridors." And on April 2, 1944, an article by Arthur Krock of the *New York Times*, examining the President's decision to permit the soldier vote bill to become law without signature, appeared under the headline of "MESSAGE ON VOTE BILL EASES CAPITOL TENSIONS. Conciliatory Tone of President Even as He Calls Measure 'Inadequate' Is Hailed as Marking a New Attitude."

A third example of the way Lambert and I attempted to demonstrate through research how the President could increase the effectiveness of his messages was the suggestion, with supporting data, transmitted to Mr. Rosenman on September 1, 1943, that the President go out of his way to admit he had made some mistakes.

In the covering letter to Mr. Rosenman we stated that "This thought of a mild admission on the part of the President is based upon the fact that most people like to have someone admit that he is slightly wrong so that they may be slightly right. Such an admission is generally followed by an emotion of understanding and tolerance and acceptance of subsequent positive statements. Our studies show a wide desire on the part of the people to have the President admit a few human failings and to minimize sarcasm in his speeches.

"If these suggested characteristics were employed in a speech, we believe they should occur coincident with the announcement by him of important war successes. These announcements should be made modestly, followed by the admission that some neglect of certain domestic policies had come about through concentration on making these successes possible."

The evidence here was based on the question: "The President has said he will soon give another radio talk about some of the problems we have here at home. Which of these two ways of talking about these problems would appeal to you most? (1) A speech like most of his former speeches in which he has his usual confident tone in discussing the problems here at home, or (2) a speech in which he frankly admits he has somewhat neglected the problems here at home because he has been busy planning for the war abroad, and asks for the public's understanding of this point?" Here, a clear majority of 53 per cent chose the second alternative, only 34 per cent choosing the first one. The wording of the question was purposely loaded against the suggestion of an "admission" by making the alternate speech completely innocuous so there could be no doubt of the point. A further question asking whether respect for the President would be increased or decreased if he did admit frankly that he had neglected problems on the home front because of his preoccupation with war plans indicated that 56 per cent would respect him more, only 7 per cent would respect him less, 32 per cent thought it would make no difference, and 5 per cent had no opinion.

Mr. Rosenman, who had recently been appointed as the President's counsel, called on September 16 to thank us for the material and to say we would see the next day some effects of our work in the President's Message to Congress on the progress of the war.

After reviewing the favorable progress of the war, the President stated:

> There have been complaints from some sources about the way this production and other domestic activities have been carried on. Some of these complaints, of course, are justified. . . .

> Fair-minded citizens, however, will realize that although mistakes have been made, the job that has been done in converting peacetime America to a wartime basis has been a great job and a successful one, of which all our people have good reason to be proud.

> It would be nothing short of a miracle if this unprecedented job of transforming a peace-loving, unprepared industrial America into a fighting and production machine had been accomplished without some mistakes being made and some people being given cause for complaint. . . .

> No sincere, sensible person doubts that in such an unprecedented, breathtaking enterprise errors of honest judgment were bound to creep in, and that occasional disputes among conscientious officials were bound to occur. And if anyone thinks that we, working under our democratic system, have made major mistakes in this war, he should take a look at some of the blunders made by our enemies in the so-called "efficient" dictatorships. . . .

> We know that in any large private industrial plant doing

a thousandth part of what their Government in Washington is doing, there are also occasional mistakes and arguments. But this is not a good comparison. It is like comparing a motor boat with a battleship. What I have said is not in any way an apology—it is an assertion and a boast that the American people and their Government are doing an amazingly good job in carrying out a vast program which two years ago was said to be impossible of fulfillment. Luckily the American people have a sense of proportion—and a memory.

The message was most favorably received. The *New York Times* wrote in an editorial the next day that "The President is entitled to a respite from the nagging of those constantly suspicious critics who magnify Darlan molehills into mountains." And *Time Magazine* of September 27, 1943, under the heading "Mr. Roosevelt at His Best" noted that "Mr. Roosevelt actually admitted that 'mistakes have been made' in Washington, admissions that from him have the rarity of pearls in restaurant oysters."

Years later, when it came time for President Eisenhower to leave the White House, I wrote on January 1, 1961, to my friend General Andrew Goodpaster, then White House staff secretary, who was awarded a Medal of Freedom by President Eisenhower the same day he gave his Farewell Address to the American people, that the President's last message before relinquishing his office might well take the form of a prayer addressed to people throughout the world as well as to the American people. The reasons I gave for this suggestion were that a message in the form of a prayer could remind people of those universal human values not bounded by time or space, or by any political or religious system; also that such a message could remind people in the non-Communist world of aspects of life threatened by Communism, just as it could (if it got behind the Iron Curtain) remind people in Communist areas of the same values. I pointed out that the world-wide respect and love for the President and the knowledge that he was a deeply religious man would provide a sincere and consistent context for such a message. I enclosed with my letter the following suggestions to include in such a prayer:

I pray that all those in want may have their needs satisfied; that all those who are underfed may be nourished; that all those who are ill or diseased may be restored to health; that all those who are denied opportunities because of their race, color, or station in life shall enjoy the advantages now available to the privileged; that all those deprived of education should be enlightened by knowledge; that all who are concerned with the welfare of children may look with confidence to the growth and development of coming generations; that all who are discouraged shall find reasons to hope; that all who yearn for freedom may experience its liberating force; that all who have freedom shall realize the responsibilities freedom entails; that all who are insensitive to the needs of others will learn charity; that all people shall live together in a peace forever guaranteed by mutual respect and love.

The President concluded his Farewell Address to the nation as follows: [21]

We pray that peoples of all faiths, all races, all nations may have their great human needs satisfied; that those now denied opportunity shall come to enjoy it to the full; that all who yearn for freedom may experience its spiritual blessings; that those who have freedom will understand, also, its heavy responsibilities; that all who are insensitive to the needs of others will learn charity; that the scourges of poverty, disease, and ignorance will be made to disappear from the earth, and that, in the goodness of time, all peoples will come to live together in a peace guaranteed by the binding force of mutual respect and love.

10

News Techniques

At various intervals during the war, considerable pressure was brought on the President and other officials to release news they thought should be withheld from the public in the interest of prosecuting the war more effectively. This pressure also came from many heads of Government news agencies who were, of course, generally men with some newspaper background.

Since Lambert and I felt that a good newspaper man often confuses, in all sincerity, the natural desire to have a good story with the question of whether the people in wartime really want that story, particularly if it is apt to endanger the lives of friends and relatives in the fighting services, we occasionally did spot-checks for the President on the state of mind of the public during periods of pressure for such news.

In late June 1942, the FBI arrested eight Nazi spies who had landed by submarine along the Atlantic Coast to engage in sabotage activities. The trial of these spies began on July 8 and, as the newspapers complained, was "shrouded in secrecy." During the trial, we conducted one of our spot-checks of 300 cases to gauge public reaction and to demonstrate that it is relatively easy to determine before a decision

is made whether or not the people will consider the withholding of certain news as unjustified censorship or as sound
news policy during wartime. The question asked was:
"Which of these statements best expresses your opinion as
to whether or not the trial should be made public: that the
trial should be reported to the public; that the decision of
whether or not to report the trial should be left up to the
person in charge of reporting news for the Government;
or, if the Army says the trial should be kept secret for military reasons, then I think it should be kept secret?"

The overwhelming majority of Americans (77 per cent)
opted for the third alternative that the trial should be kept
secret if that is the way the Army feels about it. Only 14
per cent felt it should be made public.

During the latter part of September 1942, Roosevelt made
a two weeks' trip around the country to inspect various aspects of the war effort. No advance details of the trip were
given out and he did not allow news reporters to accompany
him. Again there was considerable complaint of censorship.
Two days after the President returned to Washington, we
made a spot-check of public reaction to the secrecy maintained about the trip and immediately passed the comforting
information on to the White House. People were simply
asked whether they thought it was best to keep the President's trip a secret or allow the newspapers to report it
from the beginning. Again, the overwhelming majority
of 78 per cent elected to keep the trip secret, with only 14
per cent feeling it should have been reported, the rest having
no opinion.

Criticism that the Government was withholding up-to-the-
minute and complete news about the fighting on the Western
front mounted during the German offensive in December of
1944. We again did a spot-check of 300 cases. This indicated
once more that the great majority of American people did
not sympathize with the criticism made by newsmen of Army

authorities for refusing to allow more immediate and detailed reports of the German offensive.

The following information was handed to Miss Tully on December 27, 1944, and copies of the questions asked and the results obtained were sent to Secretaries Stimson and Forrestal. The issue involved was posed to a small sample of representative Americans as follows: "Newspaper reporters with the American armies fighting the Germans recently complained to Army officials because complete details of the fighting now going on in Germany and Belgium are being withheld from the public. The Army authorities have answered that complete reports of the fighting might help the enemy and endanger the lives of American troops. How do you feel about this? Do you think reporters should be permitted to write more complete accounts so we could all know more about the fighting, or do you think the Army authorities should withhold all information from the public whenever they think it is in the best interests of our military operations?"

Once again, the majority of the public (69 per cent) indicated their feeling that information should be withheld if Army authorities thought this was in the best interests of military operation, with only 24 per cent believing reporters should be allowed to write more complete accounts.

In addition to the problem of war-time controls on the news, there was also the problem of how to handle news releases dealing with various moot issues. For example, on the morning of March 17, 1942, came the news that General Douglas MacArthur had successfully escaped from the Philippines to Australia. Lambert and I immediately asked how the news was to be released to the public. Our question was prompted by the fact that we happened to have with us the results of a survey recently taken by the National Opinion Research Center, then directed by Harry Field, which showed that the American people were about evenly divided as to whether MacArthur should stay with his men in the Philippines to the bitter end or try to escape.

Half the public were likely, then, to be highly resentful that MacArthur had been ordered to leave, and Nazi propaganda could be counted on to exploit the action as cowardice, yellow-dog tactics, etc.

Lambert and I told an officer in the Psychological Warfare Branch of Military Intelligence how, in view of this situation, we thought the announcement should be made, and he asked us to prepare a statement. Since I had an appointment that took me out of the office, Lambert sat down and drafted the statement. It was deliberately phrased to involve all Americans in the President's decision to order MacArthur's escape and to make the decision seem the only reasonable one under the circumstances.

The statement was taken at once by the officer to Steve Early at the White House and was used verbatim by the President in the press conference that same afternoon, only a few hours after the news had been reported. The statement by the President read:

> I know that every man and woman in the United States admires with me General MacArthur's determination to fight to the finish with his men in the Philippines. But I also know that every man and woman is in agreement that all important decisions must be made with a view toward the successful termination of the war. Knowing this, I am sure that every American, if faced individually with the question as to where General MacArthur could best serve his country, could come to only one answer.[22]

Simultaneously with the news of MacArthur's arrival in Australia came the news of his appointment as Supreme Commander of the United Nations forces in the Southwestern Pacific.[23]

11

Ways to Make a Program Work

This report and those in the following two chapters illustrate the use of surveys in helping President Roosevelt learn the extent of public knowledge and awareness of certain problems with which he had to deal. Obviously, in a democracy such as ours, no President can successfully implement a policy he believes in unless the people are concerned about that policy and are educated to its implications. And the President can become a more successful educator if he knows something about the extent to which people have any information about the problems he faces and how much they are concerned with them.

On September 22, 1943, Judge Samuel I. Rosenman called Lambert and me from the White House and asked if we would come see him the next day about a problem he thought we could help with. Isador Lubin, also in the White House at the time, attended the meeting.

Judge Rosenman explained to us how those opposing the President's farm subsidy program were arguing that the farmers themselves did not want subsidies. He said that the President was puzzled as to just what the farmers' state of mind was. The President would like to know if we could find out for him.

Accordingly, we designed a study to get at the various aspects of the problem. The survey was conducted on a specially designed national sample of over 2,000 American farmers, properly distributed by region, size of farm, product, etc. We prepared a report and took it to Judge Rosenman on October 25, going over the study with him point by point before he passed it on to the President. Rosenman suggested certain changes in the order of the pages, commenting that, if the President were not interested in the first few pages of a document brought to him, he was unlikely to read the rest of it.

As usual, we included at the beginning of our report a summary of the major findings. The report contained all the data that supported the following summary:

The outstanding disclosure of this survey is the widespread ignorance of farmers with reference to the Administration's farm program, as contrasted with the apparent assumption on the part of farm groups in Washington that the farmer is well informed and has established his opinions on the basis of a clear understanding of the facts. Two of the major points of ignorance are that only 14 per cent had a clear picture of the meaning of subsidies—over half the farmers knew nothing at all. And of those who thought a guaranteed price program would cost the Government a lot of money, 58 per cent believed the money would be spent chiefly to administer the program—only 18 per cent said the money would go chiefly to farmers or middlemen to make up price differences. The survey shows that in spite of this extensive lack of information, farmers are agreed that some sort of Government regulation is essential. Less than 2 per cent cited Government control and interference as a reason for not producing the maximum. Minimum prices on farm products and ceilings on retail food prices met with general approval. Among some of the other findings are that only about 50 per cent of farmers say they are making money, and the same percentage believe they are not getting fair prices and should be guaranteed prices even if this means higher taxes for everybody. A majority believe price ceilings now will insure a better future after the war. There are only small differences between the opinions of big and little farmers.

In the letter transmitting the findings to Judge Rosenman we wrote that "In our opinion an address by the President on this subject and the reason for making it are unusual. As far as the farmer goes, we are not faced with a difference in political opinion as much as we are faced with ignorance on a subject. The primary aim, therefore, should be clarification, sacrificing, if necessary, emotional oratory for simple phrasing. Repetition is needed to assure understanding and in this case should not be feared.

"The President's lengthy and detailed message to Congress cannot be counted on to enlighten the farmers, since it will not reach the masses."

A few days after turning in the report to Judge Rosenman, Lambert and I got letters from the President commending the report as both surprising and instructive.

From its inception, Roosevelt's lend-lease policy was favored by a large majority of the American people.[24] But even though most people approved of lend-lease operations, there was considerable lack of understanding of just how they worked and what the United States was really getting back in return.

In order to find out the extent to which Americans understood the concept of "reverse lend-lease," we asked the following question on a nationwide survey in mid-September of 1943: "As far as you know, have we received any war materials and supplies from England in return for our lend-lease help?" At that time, only 25 per cent of the public answered in the affirmative, while 75 per cent either said "No" or had no opinion on the matter.

This information was transmitted to the White House on October 6, 1943, with the suggestion that the situation be clarified if possible in dramatic fashion.

About a month later, on November 11, Roosevelt informed Congress, as reported in the *New York Times*, that "Great Britain has agreed to stop taking dollars for raw materials and foodstuffs provided to us by the British Empire. Instead, he said, these contributions, as well as the shipping to deliver them, will be counted as reverse lend-lease, offsetting our lend-lease aid to the British." [25]

At the same time, in London the British Parliament was provided a detailed report of its lend-lease activities by the British Government, indicating that up to June 30, 1943, the total British Commonwealth expenditures for reverse lend-lease had amounted to $1,174,900,000. The *New York Times* headlined the story on page 1: BRITISH SUPPLY U.S. BILLION IN LEND-LEASE.

In order to check the results of these announcements, the identical question was repeated in another nationwide survey made during the latter part of November 1943. The results clearly indicated that the joint announcement had had an appreciable clarifying effect but that continued attempts needed to be made to inform the public concerning British repayment.

People were asked whether or not we in the United States had received any war materials and supplies from England in return for our lend-lease help. Results of a study made in mid-September 1943 showed that 40 per cent of the American people did not think we had received any return from England for our lend-lease help and only 25 per cent knew that we had. On the repeat study in November, the 40 per cent who did not know had dropped to 25 per cent and the earlier 25 per cent who knew had risen to 37 per cent, the rest not knowing one way or the other.

As indicated in the discussion of the trends of opinion in Chapter 7, we carefully followed the extent to which the American people distinguished between trying to negotiate a peace with the German Army, on the one hand, and with Hitler on the other. Several separate studies were made of this question at various intervals. I report only two of them here.

A memorandum was transmitted to President Roosevelt on February 16, 1943, suggesting that in one of his talks he explain briefly how the tradition and leadership of the German Army were a menace to permanent peace and how "unconditional surrender" would ensure our not being fooled by any peace terms the German Army might propose if it should oust Nazi leadership.

The supporting evidence indicated that over one-fourth of the American population still did not understand the full meaning of "unconditional surrender" and would approve discussion of peace terms with the German Army if it overthrew Hitler. And a sizable minority of the American people (21 per cent) interpreted a negotiated peace with the German Army as equivalent to a negotiated peace with the German people, who would, assumedly in a popular revolt, then be in control of the German Government.

Another memorandum on the same subject was given Miss Tully on August 9, 1944, based on a nationwide survey done the week following the attempt on Hitler's life made on July 20. It showed that a sizable minority still did not see the full implications of a peace that might be made with the German Army. The supporting data were as follows:

When asked the question "If the German Army over-throws Hitler and then offers to stop the war and discuss peace terms with the Allies, do you think we should discuss peace terms with the German Army?" 24 per cent of the people answered "yes." When asked "If the German Army actually does overthrow Hitler and the Nazi leaders, do you think this would mean that the German people would have more or less control of their government than they do now?" 43 per cent of the people answered "more," about 30 per cent answered "the same," and the rest were divided be-tween "less" and "no opinion." And, finally, when asked "If we should accept such a peace offer from the German Army, do you think we would run a greater risk of being in-volved in another world war than if we continued to fight on until the German Army was completely defeated?" about 80 per cent answered "yes," with the rest saying "no" or having no opinion.

The President repeatedly indicated in his talks and mes-sages the dangers inherent in the German military tradition. For example, in a press and radio conference held on August 17, 1944, he made it very clear that Germany would not be allowed to surrender until it was occupied by Allied troops; otherwise, he is reported to have said, "the next generation of Germans would be told that they had really won the war. . . . There is an interesting psychological study not only of the German people but of their military command, a char-acteristic to throw up the sponge when their borders are menaced because they don't want Germany overrun." [26]

12

Will Americans Support International Cooperation?

In the midst of the war, the American people as well as responsible Government leaders were thinking about the shape and design of the postwar world as they would like to see it. In order to keep the President informed of both the direction American opinion was taking and the extent to which this opinion was informed, special studies were undertaken from time to time dealing with questions of international cooperation and with some of the bases on which it was founded. Two of these reports are noted here.

The first was transmitted to the White House on December 27, 1943, and included data from a nationwide survey conducted in late November. It included, as shown in Note 27, pp. 180f., the results of questions which indicated broad public agreement that the Administration was doing a good job in handling our affairs abroad and that the American people overwhelmingly favored the establishment of some type of international organization before the war was over. The memorandum also contained the results of other questions, which indicated that the majority of the American people were uninformed about United States participation in the League of Nations and that most of them knew nothing of the "Connally Resolution," widely discussed in the press and recently passed by the Senate under the leadership of Tom Connally, then Chairman of the Foreign Relations Committee. This resolution declared in favor of an international organization, based on the principle of the sovereign equality of all peace-loving nations, to maintain peace and security.

A second example of information on this general subject was turned in to the White House on January 16, 1945, shortly before the President left for the Yalta Conference (February 3–11, 1945) with Stalin and Churchill. The memorandum was headed "An Interpretation of the State of American Public Opinion toward International Affairs." I am noting the summary as given to the White House to show the form of reporting the President liked.

Although the overwhelming majority of the American people now favor a strong international organization necessarily dominated by the big powers, it is unrealistic to assume that Americans are international-minded. Their policy is rather one of expediency, which, at the moment, takes the form of internationalism.

The present internationalism rests on a rather unstable foundation: it is recent, it is not rooted in any broad or long-range conception of self-interest, it has little intellectual basis.

Opinion is therefore susceptible to shifts or to sudden skepticism when events occur which do not easily fit into the idealistic framework people agree with and hope may be filled in.

With opinion uncrystallized and with people generally uninterested in the mechanics needed to achieve lasting peace, there is little doubt that they expect and desire strong leadership and would support the policies and mechanics the President felt necessary to achieve the ideals he has expressed, particularly if the reasons for proposed steps were made clear.

There is no question of the fact that the American people want this country to participate in an international organization with teeth in it: 92 per cent would like to see us join an international organization; 82 per cent believe every member country, including the United States, should make part of its armed forces available when necessary to stop aggression; 74 per cent think the United States, Russia, Great Britain, and China must make the major decisions in an international organization even if the small nations are dissatisfied.

A majority subscribe to certain actions that may be necessary to achieve the goals of the United Nations: 93 per cent favor continuation of food rationing if needed to provide food in formerly occupied countries; 62 per cent believe we should trade as much as possible with other countries even if it means becoming more dependent on them for some products; 62 per cent of those with opinions believe we should join an international organization even if we must compromise on the final terms of the peace settlement, as, for example, in setting boundaries; 68 per cent of those with opinions are willing to have Russia keep some Polish territory in exchange for some German territory given to Poland.

People still have comparatively little interest in or awareness of the mechanics needed to achieve the goals they hope for: 72 per cent do not feel that they have even a general idea of the Dumbarton Oaks proposals; 51 per cent have never heard or read any discussion of the Atlantic Charter; 30 per cent of the American people express no opinion on most questions dealing with the mechanics of international settlements. This is a relatively high percentage and indicates opinion is not crystallized; most people are more concerned about domestic than about international problems—the ratio is around 3 to 1.

Opinion on international affairs is highly sensitive to actions or events that seem at odds with stated ideals or which pose contingencies for which the people are unprepared. There has been a rise of 15 per cent in the past nine months (from 30 per cent to 45 per cent) in the number of people who are dissatisfied with the way in which Russia, England, and the United States are cooperating with each other. There has been a rise of 14 per cent in the past six months (from 24 per cent to 38 per cent) in the number who think other countries are taking advantage of us. There has been a rise of 17 per cent in the past six months (from 14 per cent to 31 per cent) in the number who think the British are not doing all they can to win the war.

On January 23, 1945, Raymond Daniell of the *New York Times* reported from London:

An authoritative preview of current trends of American foreign policy was given to the British Government today . . .

In substance this statement, transmitted from the White House to 10 Downing Street, was that the American people were in a mood in which the actions of their Allies could precipitate them into wholehearted cooperation for the maintenance of peace in Europe or bring about a wave of disillusionment that would make the isolation of the 1920's pale by comparison with what might follow this war. . . .

Now the British know, or at least their Government knows, that in Mr. Roosevelt's view the country gave him a mandate at the last election to play the part in world affairs that Wilson envisaged and Harding repudiated.

Although the atmosphere in the United States now is more propitious toward approval of the Dumbarton Oaks plan for international collaboration for world peace than it has ever been since 1918 toward any similar idea, the British have been told with force and authority that this mood can change as mercurially as the English weather if the American people once get the idea that this war, which started as a crusade for freedom, ends as just another struggle between rival imperialisms. . . .

A transcript of the conversation or a text of the communication delivered to Prime Minister Churchill today would be of great historical value, but unfortunately it is not available. It is possible to speculate, however, with reasonable exactitude on what was conveyed to the British Government regarding American attitudes toward developments in some parts of liberated Europe.

The British have been informed that the American people view these with disquiet and that if these continue they may bring about such a revulsion in the New World that neither Mr. Roosevelt nor anyone else could lead the people of the United States back into their present cooperative mood.[28]

Official Government interest in the state of mind of the American people concerning international affairs mounted increasingly as the war progressed. This was reflected by the creation in 1943 within the Department of State of an Office of Public Affairs and the appointment of John Sloan Dickey as its Director. John Dickey, later President of Dartmouth College, was an old friend of mine and knew of the research I was doing. He and his assistant, Shepard Jones, came up from Washington in August of 1943 to discuss the possibilities of conducting public opinion studies for the State Department that would keep it informed of public reactions and generally improve its public relations and information programs. Secretary of State Hull was completely in sympathy with the idea and had already indicated to John some subjects on which he would like to be informed.

Accordingly, we made a contract with John's new office to conduct surveys on subjects the State Department would suggest, to follow up ideas initiated by myself, and to make recommendations on how public resistances could be overcome. The contract was signed in October of 1943, and my work with the Office of Public Affairs continued for two years. During that period a number of reports were prepared for Hull personally, in addition to those sent to John's office. Even though the research was classified and cannot be reported here, it is relevant to put in the record this first official utilization of survey techniques by the Department of State.[29]

After Roosevelt's death on April 12, 1945, since the war was obviously about to end, I was eager to return to my full-time teaching and systematic research. But it was clearly important that the Office of Public Affairs continue to have facilities at its disposal, so I arranged with Harry Field, then Director of the National Opinion Research Center, to take over our contractual arrangement. Accordingly, the research contract was transferred to NORC during the summer of 1945.

13

North African Landing [30]

A number of the studies so far reported have shown the importance of understanding the state of mind of people with whom the Government must deal, at home or abroad, in order to devise the right expression of policy at the right time or to decide the right moment to act. In this and the next two chapters, I describe other suggestions of strategies that seemed likely to effect opinion in the desired directions.

On February 18, 1942, two officers from the Psychological Warfare Branch of Military Intelligence, Colonels Percy Black and Oscar Solbert, came to discuss with me in Princeton various psychological warfare problems. One of the questions they asked was whether or not I thought it feasible to try to gather any systematic information in North Africa in the event an Allied landing should be attempted in that area. At the time there was heavy fighting along the North African coast between the Nazis and Italians, under General Rommel, and the British under General Montgomery. I told Colonels Black and Solbert that, in view of the demonstrated reliability of small samples of opinion, if the cooperation of those who would have to become involved in such an undertaking could be counted on, there was a good chance we could get information of value.

Accordingly, a number of conferences were subsequently held in Washington, State Department approval for the undertaking was obtained, and I compiled a list of Americans already in North Africa representing various departments and agencies who would be both useful and highly reliable. It was felt that the safest method to get the study under way was to communicate both our intentions and our plan to some American who would shortly be coming to the United States from North Africa on routine duty and then returning. A consul, whom I shall call Robert Langrock, was due home for a short period in mid-March. Accordingly, he was conscripted for the indoctrination and came to see me in Princeton, along with Major Henry Cumming of the Psychological Warfare Branch. Mr. Langrock never visited my office but with due precaution kept himself in a room at the Nassau Tavern for the few days he was in Princeton while I explained to him the problem, the concept of sampling opinion, and how the information wanted must be obtained by indirect questioning.

Details concerning objectives, precautions, and interviewer instructions were prepared the next week in Washington with the assistance of Jerry Lambert and Major Cumming. Messages were also sent to military attachés in two other areas, indicating that they should be prepared to ask some systematic questions of a sample of people. These messages were meant to serve as blinds, in case any suspicion should be aroused about North Africa.

The initial memorandum Lambert and I submitted to Colonels Black and Solbert in late March 1942 set up three objectives for the survey: to discover, in each group of people in each district, the degrees of opposition and cooperation that might be expected in case of an invasion by a strong United States force; the causes of opposition and cooperation; and what steps would be most effective in diminishing the one and promoting the other. It prescribed a code to use if replies could not be brought back in person.

The precautions that we spelled out indicated, for example, the importance of noting differences of opinion among different groups of people interviewed and of keeping careful notations on the background and characteristics of each person interviewed. And we especially stressed the necessity of conducting all interviews in as conversational, casual, and informal a manner as possible. We suggested this indirect approach could be aided by opening the conversation with a few completely blind and irrelevant questions to be determined by the interviewer on the spur of the moment in order to get rapport with his respondent. We indicated that it was not absolutely essential to repeat the questions given the interviewer word for word, but he could lead the conversation around to those topics in which we were interested.

The questions suggested together with the supporting rationale were as follows:

A. In the long run, which side do you think will win the war, or do you think it will end in a stalemate?

B. Which side would you like to see win the war?

(This question should be a good opener. It should also reveal the fundamental desires of the respondent and indicate in a fairly innocuous way the direction his actions might take in a critical situation.)

C. (To be asked of French military and civilians):

If you could not be a Frenchman, what other country would you choose to be a citizen of?

(By judging the difficulty the respondent may have in making his answer, we may be able to evaluate his loyalty to France and gather to what extent he has already been thinking about this question. It will be important to follow the simple answer to this question with details concerning his reasons for his new choice.)

D. What do you think of the United States as a country to be a citizen of?

(This question will be asked, of course, only if the respondent has not indicated the United States in Question C. We want to find out here what respect the respondent has for the United States, what misgivings and disillusionments he may harbor, and what unfavorable attitudes the United States is encountering and should try to counteract.)

E. Do you believe the United States has some selfish and imperialistic designs on your territory, or do you think the United States has no interest in controlling this area of the world?

(Here we want to see if the respondent makes any distinction between the concept of an interdependent world operating on a cooperative basis as contrasted with the Nazi concept of an interdependent world dominated by one or two peoples.)

F. From the point of view of your own future what country's domination of this territory would be most disastrous to you personally? What would be best for you? What would be next best?

(It is important to discover, as far as possible, the very personal motivation of the respondent. How will his own military or civilian career be affected by various dominations? What domination would most upset his economic and family life, etc.?)

G. What would be your attitude if Vichy ordered resistance to any invading army?

(This is a leading question and the respondent will no doubt first say the answer to this depends on what country the invading army represents. We also want to know, if possible, if he thinks in terms of the relative strength of invading armies in determining his answers. That is, if he knew a strong German force was coming in, would he resist any more or less than if he knew a strong United States force was coming in?)

H. What do you think would be the determining factors in any military operation in your territory?

(Here we want to know if the respondent is thinking in terms of certain military factors such as superior air force, superior numbers, etc., or whether he is thinking chiefly in terms of local morale on the part of civilians, military, etc.)

The sample was designed with the help of various persons in Military Intelligence familiar with the regions involved. It was intended to follow as closely as possible the known distribution of key French military personnel. The sample we sought consisted of 68 commissioned officers, distributed by army, air force, and navy; 82 noncommissioned officers similarly distributed according to their numbers in the different armed forces; 62 civilians, and 9 native leaders—a total of 221 in all being the aim. All these groups were further distinguished by area. For the purposes of our sample, North Africa was divided into four areas which intelligence experts thought important.

Mr. Langrock returned to North Africa, indoctrinated twenty-seven reliable Americans in the purpose and method of the undertaking, and managed to return 142 detailed and useable interviews from Casablanca, Spanish Morocco, and Tangiers by July 1. The sample could not be completed because of various administrative difficulties and because of the general caution it was clearly wise to observe in many instances.

A summary of results was submitted on July 16 in a report to Military Intelligence, a copy of which was sent to the President. The following day I was asked to give members of the intelligence planning board of the General Staff an oral briefing on the whole procedure and the conclusions. The summary follows:

> In Casablanca: Among both civilian and military personnel, the majority thought the Allies would win, and almost 90 per cent wanted to see them win.

> The United States is looked on most favorably as a country to live in. Germany is regarded by 75 per cent of the people as the country whose domination of the territory would be most disastrous to them. Eighty per cent believe the United States does *not* have any imperialistic interests in French Morocco.

> If Vichy ordered resistance to an invading army, the survey shows that the majority of civilians (70 per cent) would not resist an invasion by the Allies. Among the military personnel, however, 67 per cent indicated they would resist, although there are signs that many of these would resist only half-heartedly if the invading force was strong and if Allied propaganda made it clear that the invasion was not designed for imperialistic motives but only to defeat Germany and thus help restore France.

> It is important to note that invasion by British forces would meet considerably more resistance than one composed only of United States forces. A total of 38 per cent of military and civilian personnel indicated that they would not resist the United States, would resist all except the United States, or would help the United States. Britain

is regarded unfavorably by a considerable number on several counts: traditional antagonism toward Britain and her navy, the feeling in some quarters that Britain deserted France, and mistrust of Britain's imperialistic motives.

There is also indication that an invasion force should *not* contain de Gaullists.

Some typical reports received are as follows:

French Captain. Truthful, spoke very frankly the first time I met him. A valuable source of information on native affairs, military and political. Feels should either try pre-arranging, if possible, a separatist Moroccan State here, or otherwise attempt to take Morocco by surprise (as much as possible)—Don't send English (possible exception, French Canadians) or de Gaullists—Aside from coast landings should also come down from Spanish Morocco to nullify any danger from rear—*Now* is the time to take over Morocco.

French Colonel. Truthful. Very anti-German, recognizes only hope for France is through America. Not anti-English, but anti-English foreign politics. Blames America also for her long isolation. Believes America should come here *now,* while the time is ripe. Civilians would welcome Americans, armed forces would probably start resisting, but with powerful American forces would soon and gladly give up.

French Commander. Truthful. Very nationalist. Represents the collaborationist element in the navy. Very anti-English and very suspicious of Americans now in relation to Martinique. Very anti-Russian. Cannot understand why Americans who were supposed to be friends of France can't control Martinique as they were supposed to have been doing through surveillance instead of threatening to seize it. No confidence in Anglo-Saxons after they destroyed France's security after the last war. No arguments seem to succeed in turning him from collaborationist views. He says that England has been as much of a harm to France's interest as Germany, and in any case France was beaten by Germany this time, so France might as well save what is left, even if through collaboration with Germany, because at least for the present Germany is not dismembering French Empire as are the Anglo-Saxons.

In Spanish Morocco and Tangiers: Only a small minority, 20 per cent, think the Allies will win; almost 30 per cent look for a German victory, and about 50 per cent of the population doesn't know what to think. These results become more meaningful when seen against the background of desire: almost 50 per cent of those interviewed wanted Germany to win, did not care who won, or wanted a stalemate. Those who didn't care about the outcome indicated that a clear victory for either side would be disastrous to the present Spanish government. Among the military personnel, there was great horror of Communist domination of Spain.

Only 3 per cent felt the United States had any selfish or imperialistic designs on Spanish Morocco. Domination by Germany was considered to be about as disastrous as domination by Russia. If ordered to resist an invading army, 100 per cent of the military personnel said they would obey orders, while 60 per cent of the civilians indicated they would.

Two typical comments in reply to specific questions were:

(Which side would you like to see win the war?)
Has no preference either way provided the victor does not interfere too much with Spain. States that Spain has

always been under British influence since she lost her colonies and has nothing to show for it. States it would not make much difference if Spain were under German influence for a change, but he would not like too much interference with internal matters.

(Do you believe the United States has some selfish and imperialistic design on your territory, or do you think the United States has no interest in controlling this area of the world?)

No, thinks the United States is not interested in Spanish Morocco except as a market for its goods.

The most significant finding from the study was the discovery that a landing composed solely of American ground troops would without doubt meet less resistance than an invasion that also involved British troops, because the Vichy French military personnel were suspicious that the British might have some imperialistic aims in French North Africa and they also had lingering memories of past wars with England.

In his book of memoirs, *My Three Years with Eisenhower,* Captain Harry C. Butcher noted on July 31, 1942, about two weeks after our report was submitted, that General Eisenhower's discussions with General Marshall had indicated that Churchill "looked upon the African assault as an American operation to or around Casablanca on the west coast, and as primarily a British operation on the north coast—but to be led, at the time of the landing operations, by American troops for such psychological advantages as might be gained from the French." [31]

In *The Hinge of Fate* Sir Winston Churchill cited the following message to him from Roosevelt dated August 30, 1942:

President Roosevelt to Former Naval Person

I feel very strongly that the initial attacks must be made by an exclusively American ground force, supported by your naval and transport and air units. The operation should be undertaken on the assumption that the French will offer less resistance to us than they will to the British.

I would even go so far as to say I am reasonably sure a simultaneous landing by British and Americans would result in full resistance by all French in Africa, whereas an initial American landing without British ground forces offers a real chance that there would be no French resistance, or only a token resistance.[32]

The invasion of November 7 followed this plan and met with "token resistance." The *New York Times* of November 8, 1942, began its story, dated November 7, by saying that President Roosevelt had announced that night that:

Powerful American forces, supported by British naval and air forces, landed simultaneously tonight at numerous points on the Mediterranean and Atlantic coasts of French North Africa, launching effective second front assistance to Russia and forestalling an anticipated invasion of Africa by Germany and Italy.

Since the results of the survey indicated a suspicion on the part of a number of military and civilian personnel that a successful invading army would permanently take the territory invaded away from those who then controlled it and add their country or countries to the long list of countries that at one time or another had dominated various parts of North Africa, it seemed imperative to make every effort to assure both the military and civilian personnel of North Africa that the United States had no ulterior or imperialistic designs. It had to be quite clear that the United States and her Allies were forced to take this action in order to prosecute the war successfully on behalf of France and her colonies and to prevent a German invasion and occupation of the same territory.

This point was emphasized to the Psychological Warfare Branch of Military Intelligence in July when the report of the findings was transmitted. Two concrete suggestions were offered, both based on the idea that the statement of the purpose of the invasion most credible to Frenchmen and North Africans would come from voices already well known and trusted by the French.

One of my close friends in Princeton during the war was Fernand Auberjonois, then a Swiss citizen, who was in charge of shortwave broadcasting to France for the National Broadcasting Company, who had been broadcasting to France for some time on a program which had wide coverage in France, and whose fan mail from France I had analyzed. It occurred to me that Fernand should be involved in the initial announcement of the invasion when the time came. To make a long story short, Fernand became an American citizen, an officer in the Army, and was eventually assigned to General Eisenhower's task force. He was on one of the first ships to land American troops during the invasion, a ship with special radio transmitting facilities. As the landing took place, Fernand explained it to the French, identifying himself to them in a voice they recognized.

The second suggestion was that the American voice best known and most respected in France, that of the President of the United States, should also explain to the French people in his own words, but in their language, what the landing was all about. I felt it important that a recording of the President's statement be made in advance, in case some contingency might arise. Moreover, an advance recording could be utilized by the British Broadcasting Corporation or other facilities outside the United States.

To continue with the *New York Times*'s report of the landing:

> The President made the announcement even as the American forces, equipped with adequate weapons of modern warfare, he emphasized, were making the landings.
>
> Soon he was speaking direct to the French Government and the French people by short-wave radio and in their own tongue, giving assurances that the Allies seek no territory and have no intention of interfering with friendly French, official or civilian. He called upon them to cooperate in repelling "the German and Italian international criminals."

The *Washington Star* reported some of the details of the preparation of the President's message in its issue of November 10, 1942, as follows:

> President Roosevelt was said today to have composed himself the speech in French which informed the world that our armies were taking North Africa into protective custody. . . . The President's speech was recorded under circumstances of the strictest secrecy some time ago. The actual recording was made at the White House.

The text of Roosevelt's message to the French was printed on page 1 of the *New York Times,* November 8, 1942.

Another plan, conceived about the same time as that of evaluating reactions to a North African landing, never got anywhere. At the time of their February visit to Princeton, Colonels Black and Solbert asked me how more information of military value about German morale might be obtained.

They had no definite suggestions but left the problem with me.

As I thought this over the next few days, it occurred to me that possibly a highly trained and sensitive person could be stationed in each of the neutral capitals around Germany to gather useful information in a systematic way. The type of person I had in mind was one who knew something about analyzing radio broadcasts from Germany; who knew how to devise indirect questions that might be revealing if asked of German civilians or military personnel visiting neutral areas; who knew something about the sampling of opinion so any information gathered could be put in context, if possible, along with similar types of information obtained in one way or another from different population groups representative of the German people; and, finally, someone who could handle himself in potentially tight and tricky situations.

In the aftermath of Pearl Harbor, Lloyd Free was beginning to feel that he should be taking a more active part in the war, so I immediately thought of him as a person ideally qualified to carry out the first experiment. Lloyd was receptive to the idea and I introduced him to Colonels Black and Solbert in their office on February 25. They were enthusiastic about following through and having Lloyd join the Army to try the idea out in Berne, Switzerland. The thought was that, if Lloyd found the notion feasible, five other people would be sought and trained for similar assignments elsewhere. Lloyd was soon given a commission in the Army. The hope at the time was that, shortly after Lloyd got to his destination, the proper radio receiving equipment together with a few German-speaking assistants could be sent to him. We at home base would try to send him assistants who had some training and he would give them further indoctrination on the spot.

Lloyd finally managed to obtain a visa from the Vichy

government to travel through France and took off on a Clipper from New York on April 28, 1942. After he got to Berne, he communicated his needs to Washington a number of times by letter and cable but got no reply, no explanation for the silence, and no assurance the original plan would be put into operation. Then in November 1942, when the North African invasion was launched and the Germans took over Vichy France, he was surrounded, and no equipment or personnel could be got to him even if someone had tried.

It was learned later that what had frustrated the original plan was a jurisdictional squabble in Washington as to who was to conduct the sort of psychological intelligence in which he was meant to engage. The Psychological Warfare Branch of Military Intelligence lost the battle (the Office of War Information won it), so Lloyd was left stranded in Berne, where he spent the duration of the war carrying out customary military intelligence duties as an assistant military attaché.

14

Postwar Policy

Many studies of American opinion during the first few years of World War II had indicated the possibility of a strong underlying feeling throughout the country that considerable opposition could arise if aid were given to other nations after the war at the sacrifice of our own needs and comforts.

Since the importance of international cooperation was so overwhelming that no form of resistance in the public mind could safely be neglected if mass approval was to be obtained, a study was undertaken to discover the attitude of the public towards postwar international affairs as compared with domestic affairs. With this information, the ultimate and practical success of the Administration's plans for permanent peace might more surely be obtained. Accordingly, a nationwide survey was conducted in mid-October of 1943.

The results of the study were transmitted in the usual form to the President through Judge Rosenman on November 15, 1943. The memorandum was deliberately brief. The data giving supporting evidence are contained in Note 33, pp. 182 to 185.

The results of the survey indicated that people are almost

twice as much interested in domestic affairs as in international affairs; that two-thirds of the people think we should not give aid to foreign countries after the war if this would lower our own standard of living; and that almost half the people think that if we do aid foreign countries after the war, our own standard of living will be lowered.

We recommended that, solely as a method of obtaining public support for its international plans, the Administration should carefully avoid giving the impression to the nation that foreign affairs will be carried on at the expense of domestic progress, and that wherever possible, in all public statements, the Administration should tie all references to international cooperation clearly and closely to the public's own self-interest here at home. Further, we pointed out that the people's ultimate welfare would be further advanced by international cooperation than by inaction on our part.

In his annual Message to Congress on January 11, 1944, the President heavily stressed the home front and spelled out in detail what he meant by his "economic Bill of Rights":

> . . . We have come to a clear realization of the fact that true individual freedom cannot exist without economic security and independence. "Necessitous men are not free men." People who are hungry and out of a job are the stuff of which dictatorships are made.
>
> In our day these economic truths have become accepted as self-evident. We have accepted, so to speak, a second Bill of Rights under which a new basis of security and prosperity can be established for all, regardless of station, race, or creed.
>
> Among these are:
>
> The right to a useful and remunerative job in the industries or shops or farms or mines of the nation;

The right to earn enough to provide adequate food and clothing and recreation;

The right of every farmer to raise and sell his products at a return which will give him and his family a decent living;

The right of every business man, large and small, to trade in an atmosphere of freedom from unfair competition and domination by monopolies at home or abroad;

The right of every family to a decent home;

The right to adequate medical care and the opportunity to achieve and enjoy good health;

The right to adequate protection from the economic fears of old age, sickness, accident, and unemployment;

The right to a good education.

All of these rights spell security. And after this war is won we must be prepared to move forward, in the implementation of these rights, to new goals of human happiness and well-being.

And in approaching the problem of aid to other nations, Roosevelt clearly tied this in with the country's own welfare:

There are people who burrow through our nation like unseeing moles, and attempt to spread the suspicion that if other nations are encouraged to raise their standards of living, our own American standard of living must of necessity be depressed.

The fact is the very contrary. It has been shown time and again that if the standard of living of any country goes up, so does its purchasing power—and that such a rise encourages a better standard of living in neighboring countries with whom it trades. That is just plain common sense . . .

It is our duty now to begin to lay plans and determine the strategy for the winning of a lasting peace and the establishment of an American standard of living higher than ever before known. We cannot be content, no matter how high the general standard of living may be, if some fraction of our people—whether it be one-third or one-fifth or one-tenth—is ill-fed, ill-clothed, ill-housed, and insecure . . .[34]

15

U.S. Propaganda in Germany

This and the next two chapters describe instances of the way in which the plausibility or credibility of communications designed to achieve a certain objective can be tested. The basic idea is that it is possible by means of research to design more effective ways of talking to people about the point of view one is trying to get across and lessen the time, energy, and money wasted in scattered efforts to influence people with arguments that do not get their attention or do not ring true to them. All three of these studies utilized small samples of the population, the reliability of which was pointed out in Chapter 4.

In February 1942, as Jerry Lambert and I worked with the Psychological Warfare Branch of Military Intelligence on the North African study and other ventures, the rather obvious idea occurred to us that some time we should try to devise a mechanism for tapping German civilian opinion as a guide to the plausibility of our information and propaganda lines. But an idea of this sort, we knew, would need strong support from the top. So we mentioned it to no one until there seemed to be some realistic hope of carrying it off.

By September of 1943, we felt that the President and various of his aides had sufficient confidence in us to be interested and to pass the suggestion along to the officials who would be most involved. On September 2, 1943, the White House called General William J. ("Wild Bill") Donovan, then head of the Office of Strategic Services (OSS), asking if he would see us on a matter of interest to the White House. Lambert and I had a long lunch at Donovan's home the next day and found him enthusiastic about the idea of obtaining a systematic study of German opinion. He offered to help us in any way.

Since the cooperation of the Office of War Information (OWI) would also be required in gathering data, we waited for the return from London of Mr. Wallace Carroll, since he was at the time Deputy Director of Overseas Operation for OWI and the appropriate person in the organization to pass judgment on our proposal. We saw him in February of 1944, and he too was enthusiastic about the plan. He offered to provide whatever OWI facilities might be available to interview Germans visiting neutral countries as well as German prisoners of war.

It was also essential that we get at least the tacit blessing of the State Department for the operation. Arrangements were made for us to see Secretary of State Edward R. Stettinius, Jr. He approved the idea, assured us he would put no obstacles in the way, but pointed out the various reasons why the State Department facilities could not be used for such an undertaking. Among these reasons was fear of the Department's involvement in something that might backfire in postwar settlements and former Secretary Hull's rigid rule that the diplomatic pouch not be used for any nefarious business. It was, of course, a great relief to have State Department approval.

By early March of 1944 we were ready to see Bill Donovan

again. He said he would instruct some of the people the OSS infiltrated into Germany to ask the questions we proposed. Thus we had three potential sources of information: interviews with civilians inside Germany, interviews with Germans traveling to neutral countries, and German prisoners of war.

After many more discussions with Wally Carroll in Lambert's home in Washington, we decided the information most useful to the United States propaganda effort at that time would be answers to two questions: First, was it plausible to try to make the German people aware that the trend of the war was going against them or reinforce this idea among those who already harbored it? Second, could we erase some of the sting of the phrase "unconditional surrender," which Roosevelt had used, by convincing the German people that the term applied only to top government officials and would not mean enslavement, imprisonment, or disaster for civilians themselves? As General Eisenhower indicated years later, Roosevelt's slogan of "unconditional surrender" appeared to be aimed at peoples rather than at the warlords who led them.[35]

In addition to these two questions, we decided to include a question that tapped what we ourselves believed would be a highly implausible idea and that would serve as a control on the interviews. If answers to such a question differed from our expectations, then, we felt, the whole study would be suspect. The question we introduced for this purpose dealt with the possibility of a successful internal revolt against present German leadership.

By the end of the first week of March, Lambert and I had prepared a memorandum on our proposal, an explanation of the procedure to be followed, and the questions together with their rationale. These were transmitted to Donovan and Carroll, who then took over and sent instructions to the people who would be involved in the research.

Only a few points emphasized in the instructions need be mentioned here. We pointed out that the system used in this investigation differed from ordinary intelligence methods in that we sought brief and specific information on clearly defined subjects, not a mass of incidental and random information. We insisted that all information be obtained through casual conversation to avoid any suspicion on the part of those interviewed. We provided suggestions for indirect conversational approaches that would be likely to elicit the type of information we wanted. We pointed out it was essential that complete background data be obtained about everyone interviewed, that all the material gathered be pooled so that no one interviewer should feel it essential to obtain a representative sample himself. We emphasized that no agent should ever try to make a report fit the pattern of any previous information or ever allow his own thoughts to alter the literal reporting of the actual replies received.

The first interviews began coming in by cable early in April, some through Donovan's office, others through Carroll's office, reporting the opinions of Germans traveling in Sweden, Turkey, Switzerland, and Portugal, as well as of some prisoners of war in England. All conversations on which our results were based took place before D-Day on June 6, and most of them were in our hands by that time. By early July, Lambert and I felt we had all the results we could get: eighty-seven cases in all, a small sample indeed but still rather remarkable considering the circumstances and the competing demands on the time of those who did the interviewing for our study. In addition to the interviews obtained in Germany, qualified persons working with OWI or OSS talked to Germans who had recently left their country and who were interviewed in Stockholm, Istanbul, Berne, Lisbon, or England.

Seventy-eight conversations were held directly with Germans, nine with Swedish observers who had just talked to Germans. The sample included persons from various occupational groups, all age groups, of different educational levels, and with varying attitudes toward the Nazi party. Many were lukewarm toward the Nazis; about one-fourth could be classified as ardently pro-Nazi. We made no claim that this sample was truly representative of the German population. However, the internal consistency of the opinions of different types of persons interviewed, both inside and outside Germany, indicated high reliability. Except for a few Germans who appeared ignorant and unconcerned and the minority who were blind Nazi followers, all answers appeared to be thoughtful and were regarded by the observers who obtained them as reliable expressions of opinion.

We prepared our report and submitted a copy to Wally Carroll on July 13, 1944, also handing a copy that day to Grace Tully in the White House. The President wrote us a note of thanks.

Our summary of the results of the survey indicated that both the propaganda lines emphasizing trend and the theme of minimizing the personal consequences to civilians of unconditional surrender would be plausible and effective. Since these reactions were obtained before the invasion, they were undoubtedly conservative as of the time of the report.

Here are the specific results as contained in the report:

1. *Are the Germans conscious of the trend against them?* Thirty-two per cent think the present trend will continue and Germany will be defeated; 29 per cent believe the present trend is going against Germany and, if the invasion from England succeeds, Germany will lose the war; 20 per

cent feel the present trend against Germany is only temporary; 5 per cent say the war will end in a stalemate; 9
per cent are unaware of any trend or believe there is no unfavorable trend; 5 per cent gave no information.

It should be noted here that of those who answered the
question only 10 per cent were unaware of the present
trend against Germany. Combining the answers of those who
already see Germany defeated and those who say the invasion will decide shows that well over half of those questioned (61 per cent) were clearly pessimistic about Germany's chances.

This figure rises slightly when prisoners of war are excluded: 58 per cent of all other Germans feel the war is already lost, and this figure rises to 66 per cent when those
who see the invasion as a test are added. Older people are
more pessimistic than the young. Even most of those who
are definitely pro-Nazi appear defeatist: only about one-third
regard the present trend as temporary. The only people unaware of the present trend against Germany were persons
whom the observers described as ignorant and unconcerned
about anything but their own immediate personal welfare.
Except for the greater emphasis prisoners of war placed on
the outcome of the invasion, the opinions of Germans con-
tacted at many points and by many different observers were
consistent as to the war's outcome.

2. *What does the phrase "unconditional surrender" mean
to the German people—do they think it means complete
disaster for them as individuals?* Seven per cent never
heard of the phrase (all of these were prisoners of war);
26 per cent said they were fearful of the consequences of
surrender to Russia, but were not worrying much about possible surrender to the Western powers because they would
expect relatively good treatment and personal freedom from

them; 18 per cent believed there would be virtual enslavement and that all normal life would be destroyed for them; 11 per cent felt the Allies would exploit German industry and resources but that there would still be a good chance for individuals to get along; 10 per cent said surrender would mean capitulation only of the leaders and would not be bad for the people themselves; 10 per cent believed there would be fair treatment for the Germans with a good chance to carry on normal life; 5 per cent were especially fearful of internal chaos and revenge from foreign workers now in Germany; 13 per cent gave no information.

It is important to note that over half of those who thought unconditional surrender meant virtual enslavement were among the small group classified as blind followers of the Nazis. The more thoughtful persons tended to be particularly worried about the consequences of surrender to Russia. And it was among the most thoughtful Germans and the Swedish observers that the fear of internal chaos and revenge was expressed.

The control question received a very low rating from all observers, thus lending credence to the reliability of the opinions reported on the two key questions: 86 per cent believed any overthrow would be impossible; 11 per cent felt the army might overthrow the Nazi rulers if conditions got sufficiently bad; 3 per cent thought a Communist revolution was conceivable.

The two approaches tested and found plausible, that Germans could be made aware of the trend against them and that they could be convinced that "unconditional surrender" did not refer to civilians, became part and parcel of our official propaganda line. In an editorial of October 13, 1944, the *New York Times,* for example, made the following observation:

There may be little present hope of a revolt against the Gestapo, but the American commander before Aachen invites such revolt when he makes it clear once more that "unconditional surrender" is a military term to be applied to the German war machine. Demanding such surrender, he assures the civilian population that "we Americans do not wage war against innocent civilians," and General Eisenhower himself emphasizes again that we shall "treat the Germans justly and in conformity with civilized standards." That is not only good psychological warfare; it conforms with the declarations made by Allied statesmen. It is Hitler who wages a war of extermination, and now he is waging it against the German people themselves.

In a discussion on March 24, 1944, Wallace Carroll posed to Lambert and me an interesting propaganda problem he was wrestling with at the time. He asked for any suggestions we might have. The problem was to see if any propaganda pressure could be exerted to get the *Luftwaffe* in the air before D-Day so its fighting strength could be reduced. Taunts and challenges had failed to bring up German fighter planes in sufficient numbers to be effectively attacked.

After some discussion, the idea emerged that our news sources, with their high reliability, should simply point out that American experts and the American people were confused as to the exact course the German Army planned to pursue with respect to our bombing of Germany. The alternatives were clear: either the *Luftwaffe* would be sent up to try to destroy our bombers, or German civilians and German industry would continue to be pounded without protection. It looked to us Americans, the news would report, that the German government had decided to save the *Luftwaffe* and let civilians and industry be destroyed instead. We Americans proposed to give the German people our impressions on the dilemma from time to time, etc. The idea, of course, was to create civilian pressure for more protection.

Mr. Carroll has written that his directive along these lines "was approved by the representatives of the Chiefs of Staff and the air forces at the Planning Board meeting of March 28." [36]

16

U.S. Propaganda in Italy and Holland

By early 1951, I had become increasingly disturbed by what appeared to me the lack of any sensible, systematic theme in the Government's information and propaganda programs for people in other countries. In other words, before trying to get across an idea to people abroad, we ought to ask ourselves, what should the emphasis be? How do the people we are trying to influence see the problem in their own terms? What difference does it make in their own lives? How does the idea relate to their own purposes?

It should be emphasized that testing the plausibility of appeals definitely does not require policy to be altered or tailored in any way, nor does it involve any tricky strategy. It is simply an intelligent method of framing an approach by ascertaining the psychological context within which the message will be received.

Since I had been unable to persuade anyone in the regular information services to try out the idea, in the spring of 1951 I again went to my friend Dave Niles in the White House and sought his advice. Dave said the person in the Administration most likely to understand the value of such an approach was Averell Harriman, then on the White House staff as Director of the Mutual Security Agency. Dave made an appointment for me to see Harriman the next morning. Mr. Harriman became so interested in the idea that, after discussion in the morning, he phoned Edward W. Barrett, then Assistant Secretary of State, asking if he could come over to talk with us after lunch. The upshot was that Ed Barrett got $35,000 for me to experiment with the idea. The money was made available to the Institute for Associated Research, of which I was president.

I decided to test appeals in two countries, Italy and Holland, which presented markedly different problems to the United States. I knew that in both of these countries research facilities were available to do the job well. Accordingly, I went to Bellagio, Italy, to meet with Jan Stapel, Director of the Netherlands Institute of Public Opinion, and Dr. Pierro Luzzato-Fegiz, Director of The Institute for Statistical and Public Opinion Research in Italy, to discuss the idea and the details of the research they were to undertake for me.

In the final report, submitted in June 1952, the purposes of the study were described as those of discovering the state of mind of a nation; devising a variety of possible appeals based on the state of mind discerned in each nation; finding out which appeals are most credible; and then measuring the impact of these appeals on the public opinion of a nation.

Each study was to be based on carefully selected cross-sections of 500 people in each of the countries studied, Holland and Italy. All people were first to be interviewed with a series of questions designed to uncover their opinions about the United States and its intentions abroad, about the Soviet Union and Communism, and about their own standards of living and prospects for a good life.

The second step in the research was to devise eleven different appeals on the basis of what we had learned concerning the opinions of the people in Holland and Italy. In order to make the test realistic, the appeals all related to a major United States policy, the promotion of NATO. The eleven appeals were each contained in a short paragraph that could be the gist of a speech the next President of the United States might give. Each appeal was printed on a separate card.[37]

All persons interviewed were asked to rate "How much you think this type of speech would convince most Italians (Hollanders)?" and a simple rating device known as a Scalometer, designed by Jan Stapel, was used to get reactions. The Scalometer device shows ten boxes in a vertical column on a card, with five boxes marked with a plus above a mid-line and five marked minus below it, the top box being most favorable, the bottom most unfavorable. The respondent simply points to the box that best represents his feeling.

The eleven appeals together with the ratings assigned them were as follows. The number following each appeal represents the sum (subtracting minuses from pluses) assigned on the Scalometer rating by all respondents, after adjusting to a base of 100. The maximum score possible was 500; the minimum, minus 500.

Relative acceptance of appeals in Italy and Holland

	ITALY	HOLLAND
The idea of a better tomorrow in general	153	198
Individual dignity and freedom	151	236
The idea of a better tomorrow for everyone in the world as envisioned by the American people	143	121
European Union	137	163
Soviet threat to independence	132	245
Peace	124	158

	ITALY	HOLLAND
Become strong as a nation for own self-interest	114	149
Democracy	86	190
National pride	84	207
Fear of domination by the United States	56	102
Europe must do more for itself since the United States is overburdened	10	94

It can be seen from the results that there are marked differences in the various themes both within each country and between the two countries. In Holland we found comparative satisfaction with the current standard of living, whereas in Italy there was at the time widespread dissatisfaction and an acute awareness of poverty, overpopulation, hunger, and job uncertainty; in Holland there was an overwhelming belief that Communism is bad and that Soviet propaganda claims were false, whereas in Italy, while a sizable minority were attracted to Communism, they feared its consequences for Italian independence.

As a final part of the study but one which was not provided for in the contract, we ran a small test in Holland. A hypothetical speech was written which wove together the three appeals most effective in Holland. The speech, which follows, was designed to promote NATO and was said to have been given by Mayor McBride of Ann Arbor, Michigan.

Hollanders have every right to be proud of their country. They are proud too, and quite rightly so, of the Dutch contributions to Western civilization in the past.

And Hollanders also are rightly proud that their country still makes important daily contributions and continues to play its own role in what happens in the world.

We Americans are and will continue to be grateful for what the Netherlands has done for the foundation and growth of the United States.

It is due also to Dutch influences that we here in America, just as the people of Holland, know that government is meant for the citizens.

We know that the purpose of government is the defense of human dignity. And the protection of the individual freedom of every human being.

Every government, whether it be in America or in Holland, must give every man and woman the best chances to realize his or her own plans for the future.

This is not the case everywhere. Czechoslovakia and Korea have demonstrated that the type of government and society we want is in danger.

The men who run the Soviet Union have shown they haven't any respect for a man's independence. Nor for the independence of a country.

The nations of Europe could easily be conquered one after another if they had to defend themselves all alone.

That is why the strong alliance of the Atlantic Pact is such a good and necessary thing. Our self-interest and our highest principles both show how important it is that all nations of free Western Europe and of North America have united in the Atlantic Pact.

United they are strong. Each alone is weak. Together in the Atlantic Pact they will know how to protect their freedom and independence.

The Netherlands Institute of Public Opinion mailed printed copies of the speech to *half* the people who had been interviewed on the first phase of the study. A few days later, *all* people who had been interviewed on the first phase of the study received a short questionnaire by mail asking two of the questions they had already answered a few months earlier. We could then compare the opinions of people who had received the speech with the opinions of those who had not received the speech.

When the control group that was not sent the speech was compared with the experimental group that did receive the speech on the question "What do you think about Holland's participation in the North Atlantic Pact?" by asking them to indicate their opinion on the Scalometer, the results showed a shift of over 100 points in the experimental group and an insignificant twenty points in the control group. And when the two groups were asked "What do you think: Does America's rearming increase or decrease the chances of war?" among the experimental group, the average percentage who felt America's rearming increased the chances of war fell by 24 per cent but remained constant in the control group.

It is clear that the people who received the speech became more favorable toward Holland's participation in NATO and that, irrespective of their original opinions about the chances of involvement in war due to America's rearming, there was a significant change of opinion only among those who read the speech. These results are particularly significant since the speech was only sent in the mail without any build-up or repetition and without any authoritative sponsorship.

The report concluded by pointing out that the plausible appeals method has general applicability. If this technique, adapted according to the situation, were put to full use, whether for a Presidential speech, an ambassador's conversation, a leaflet, a poster, or a radio program, the United States Government could influence public opinion in other countries much more effectively.

The report was submitted to Ed Barrett and was distributed to a number of people in the Government as well as to some of my interested friends. A copy also went later to Secretary of State John Foster Dulles, who was a close friend as well as a Princeton classmate of Lambert's. The report was deliberately written for nonspecialists, in such a way that the point of the experiment could be easily and quickly understood.

17

Appeals to Voters in France and Italy

One of the first studies I made under the aegis of the Institute for International Social Research was concerned with people in France and Italy who voted Communist in protest against their situation in life. At that time (1955–57), little was known about the assumptions, concerns, worries, and aspirations of such protest voters. The study appeared under the title, *The Politics of Despair*.[38]

In attempting to get a better understanding of the state of mind of the protest voters, I felt, again, that inquiry concerned with the plausibility of appeals would tell us something useful about how stable, intense, or fixed the points of view of the protest voters were. Did any contrary arguments make sense to them? If so, would these arguments in any way alter their opinions? Behind this query was also the hope that if a more reasonable approach could be demonstrated it might be utilized by those responsible for United States communications, particularly by the Secretary of State, to the French and Italian people.

To find answers to these questions, I conducted an experiment in France and another in Italy, using the same general procedure in each case. First, I obtained opinions from a sample of people who had voted Communist concerning a specific issue related to their protest vote. These voters were then given an argument or "approach" to read. Since I was interested in testing the relative effect of different approaches, I devised several different arguments pointing to the same conclusion. Each approach was printed as though it were an excerpt from an American newspaper and was shown to a small sample of protest voters. Each of the samples used to test each of the approaches was as similar as possible to the other samples used for the other approaches. Next, I found out how reasonable or plausible the voters thought each of the arguments was, using the Scalometer device described on page 110. Finally, I questioned the voters again on the issue selected for the first step.

Since I wanted to test the method in one country before proceeding to another, the experiments were not made simultaneously. The first was conducted in France in March 1956, and then, the following August, after the French results were evaluated, the experiment was carried out in Italy. On the basis of the French experience, the approaches were reduced in number from five to four in Italy and were somewhat modified.

However, an important difference between the two tests was in the choice of issue. In France, I tested the opinion of the United States held by the protest voters, and the aim of the arguments was to explain the United States line against Communism. In Italy, on the other hand, the opinion tested concerned the confidence of the protest voters in their government, the degree of confidence they would have in a government headed by Togliatti, the Communist Party leader, as Prime Minister, and the degree of confidence they would have in a government with Nenni, the left-wing Socialist Party leader, as Prime Minister. In this case, the arguments were designed to point out the potentially dangerous consequences of voting for Communism. The experiment in France, then, dealt with an issue about which there was a certain ambivalence: an issue that was relatively distant, impersonal, and unimportant to the protest voter. The Italian experiment, on the other hand, dealt with an issue which was obviously of more immediate concern to the voters themselves: an issue about which one might expect a relatively stable opinion, not to be greatly altered by words alone.

The Experiment in France

1. *Similarity of Goals.* Here I tried to point out that the people of France and the people of America both wanted to achieve the goals all human beings seek: a better standard of living, respect for individual rights and privileges, and greater opportunity for personal development; that the material well-being of the United States was basically due to our deep concern for the welfare of all people; and that Communism threatened the realization of these common goals.

2. *Domination vs. Freedom.* Here the thesis was that the fundamental choice facing people today was not a choice between capitalism or socialism, as the Soviet leaders made out, but a choice between domination versus freedom to develop any system desired. In this approach I tried to show that capitalism in the United States was not the kind of system the French Left thought it was. I emphasized the control placed on American capitalism, the increasingly widespread distribution of wealth, the friendship of the United States with socialist countries, and the threat to the freedom of the people which Soviet domination of any country poses.

3. *How to Achieve a Perfect Society.* Here I deliberately tried to sympathize with the Communist vision of a more perfect social order, but argued, on the one hand, the disadvantages of having this order prescribed by a few individuals in a position of absolute power and, on the other hand, the advantages of the democratic system, under which people could themselves decide on the best means to achieve a better society.

4. *United States Self-Interest.* This approach was based on two points in the American credo: that man has a right to freedom that permits him to participate in his own destiny and that people are justified in trying to repel any attempts to take this freedom away. In this sense, it was argued, American aid to others is selfish, since America believes the Soviets are trying to take away such freedom.

5. *"Official" United States Line.* This consisted of a description of what appeared to be the official explanation of United States policy towards Communism. This fifth approach was used as a control. It paraphrased certain paragraphs taken from a statement of Secretary of State John Foster Dulles at Karachi on March 6, 1956. It reported how Soviet propaganda deliberately gave a distorted view of American life, what the United States really stands for, and how the Soviet Union took every opportunity to use its power to subjugate other people and turn other nations into colonies.

Results

The shift of opinion resulting from each of the five approaches was calculated simply by comparing the average rating of opinion concerning the United States before and after respondents had read the approach. The results are shown on the following chart.

Shift in Percentage Points in Average Ratings on Different Approaches

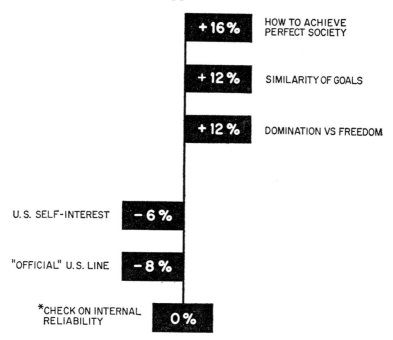

+16% HOW TO ACHIEVE PERFECT SOCIETY

+12% SIMILARITY OF GOALS

+12% DOMINATION VS FREEDOM

U.S. SELF-INTEREST −6%

"OFFICIAL" U.S. LINE −8%

*CHECK ON INTERNAL RELIABILITY 0%

* This is based on interviews with a separate group of protest voters who were not shown any appeal at all but were asked to give their ratings at the beginning of the interview and then, aften a long series of questions, to give their ratings again.

It will be seen from this chart that three of the approaches effected a much more favorable opinion of the United States, while two of them had a negative effect.

The Experiment in Italy

In our first approach, we acknowledged the many legitimate grievances of Italian workers: their low standard of living, the widespread unemployment, their unfulfilled aspirations, etc. We deplored the social injustice they suffered, the broken promises they had experienced, and sympathized with their feeling that none of the recent Italian Center governments had concerned itself primarily with workers' problems. We pointed out that one of the alternatives open to Italian workers was to give strong support to a non-Communist democratic party, which, once it recognized that they were the source of its strength, would be compelled to improve the lot of the workers as quickly as possible; that, until something like this happened, of course the promises of the Communists to carry out drastic reforms would be attractive. We said that the Italian workers themselves knew very well the threat to their independence that Communism presented; that Communism in Italy tended to follow the dictates of Moscow; and so on.

The other three approaches were similar to the second, third, and fifth appeals used in France.

Results

Not a single one of the four approaches used in Italy affected opinion to any appreciable degree. There was the same uniform lack of confidence in their current government after the argument was presented as before; and the rather uniform confidence expressed in a government that might be headed by Togliatti or Nenni was also unaffected. However, there was a significantly different rating of the reasonableness or plausibility of the four arguments used. The two rated least implausible were those concerned with the perfect society and the different ways of attaining it and the arguments sympathizing with the political problems faced by the Italian worker. The least plausible argument was that paraphrasing the then official explanation of United States policy.

The relatively fluid state of opinion about the United States among the protest voters in France contrasted sharply with the highly rigid, firmly grounded opinions held by Italian protest voters concerning their Center government and governments that might be headed by the then leader of the Communist Party or the leader of the leftist Socialist Party. No doubt the reason for this contrast was that the Italian protest voter had more confidence in Communism than the French protest voter. The number of card-holding Party members in Italy was estimated to be nearly two million but in France no more than half a million, even though Italy's population was only about 12 per cent greater than France's. In Italy, of course, there was no strong middle-class tradition, such as existed in France, and no real democratic tradition to appeal to. The relative poverty, the unemployment, and the burgeoning population were also important factors in the Italian protest vote. A second reason for the results of the tests given in Italy was certainly the fact that the tests there dealt with subjects that had much greater meaning for the respondents than the subjects of the tests used in France had for the French: Italians have obviously had infinitely more experience with Italian politics and Italian political parties than they or the French have had with the United States and international affairs.

It is, therefore, clear that the protest voter sees the world in terms of his personal experience and of the psychological consequences which social, economic, and political events have had for him; also that his view of the world is not readily subject to change by logical, intellectual approaches.

Nevertheless, the experiments did demonstrate that, with a little systematic effort, it is possible to understand the world of the protest voter well enough to find ways to talk to him effectively about issues and problems on which he has no firm opinion. The three approaches that appealed to the French protest voters were those couched in terms consistent with their view of the world, their dream of a more perfect society, their fear of losing the freedom they had by submerging themselves in a revolutionary movement, and their desire to enjoy some of the comforts and privileges of middle-class life. The two approaches that did not make sense to the French protest voters and actually influenced them in an unfavorable direction were those which confirmed their unfavorable judgments of the United States: its selfishness, its self-righteousness, and its blind, blustering antagonism to anything labeled Communist.

The results of the experiments indicate that people in one country (in this case Americans) cannot effectively communicate with important segments of the people in other countries (in this case the protest voters in France and Italy) if they think only in terms that are significant to themselves and make no effort to understand the meanings that people in other lands attach to the same terms. Although any sophisticated person is intellectually aware of this fact, such knowledge by no means guarantees or seems even to affect the search for and the use of ways of communicating with other peoples in terms of their own experience.

Of course, arguments or approaches alone can never be a substitute for programs of substantive action. Far from it. But the discovery of the right approaches to other peoples on certain issues of mutual concern at least provides a greater chance that our actions will not be made ineffective by our failure to recognize and try to overcome whatever psychological barriers separate us.

After the results were in and long before the study was published, Lambert and I went to see Secretary of State John Foster Dulles to go over the method and the results with him. We pointed out that the type of appeal he was using rated lower than any of the other appeals that had been devised and that, in fact, in France the approach he was taking seemed to have a slightly negative effect. Dulles was interested in the procedure and the results but there was certainly no indication in his subsequent statements that he took any of the suggestions seriously. Dulles once said in a conversation that "If I so much as took into account what people in other countries are thinking and feeling, I would be derelict in my duty as Secretary of State."

18

UNESCO's "Tensions Project"

It is a truism to say that people all over the world crave peace just as it is to point out that no people ever seem to feel that their own government commits aggression. In this and the next three chapters, I report on some studies designed to improve our understanding of people in other lands and of people in general so that dialogues between peoples might become more effective, inflammatory statements be discouraged, and international cooperation promoted by taking into account a few basic psychological observations.

In December of 1947, Julian Huxley, in his capacity as Director-General of UNESCO (United Nations Educational, Scientific and Cultural Organization), called me from Paris to ask if I would be willing to organize a research program that had been authorized at the second meeting of the UNESCO General Assembly. The purpose of the various resolutions that constituted what came to be labeled "The Tensions Project" was to enlist the services of social scientists in a study of "Tensions Affecting International Understanding."

I was sent information about the intended project, saw

various Americans then involved with UNESCO affairs, and after a good deal of soul-searching decided to undertake the assignment, but only for a six months' period. Since I was just beginning the research program with Del Ames referred to in Chapter 3, I did not want to be away from it longer than that. But the challenge of launching such a program from scratch was too great to turn down completely. Accordingly, arrangements were made to take leave from the University for a semester, the family was packed up with huge boxes of supplies because of the shortages still obtaining in France, and I assumed my duties in March 1948.

I shall never forget the first few minutes in the office assigned me at UNESCO House, once the palatial Hotel Majestic, on Avenue Kléber. The office had apparently been a huge dressing room, with mirrors completely covering all four walls. It contained a large desk with a fresh blotter, sharpened pencils, a mimeographed copy of the five resolutions constituting the Tensions Project, and a budget of $100,000 for the year. Later, I sat at the desk a good many hours wondering just how and where to start. Sir Julian Huxley, Walter Laves, Deputy Director of UNESCO, and two veteran, dedicated UNESCO associates, P. W. Martin and Arvid Brodersen, were most helpful in those early days as well as throughout all phases of the project.

One of the lessons I learned very quickly was that the term "social science" meant quite different things to the French, the British, and the Americans who had largely instigated the idea in the UNESCO General Assembly. The French emphasis was on the legal approach, the British emphasis on an historical approach, and both groups had to be tactfully indoctrinated in the meaning of modern social science. Another problem I faced immediately was the necessity of utilizing social scientists from as wide a variety of UNESCO-member nations as possible, when, as a matter of fact, in most of these nations there simply were not at the time many competently trained social scientists. But we finally managed to work out and get agreement on a number of different projects.[39] I shall mention here only two of them.

One of the resolutions of the General Assembly read: "An inquiry into the influences which predispose towards international understanding on the one hand and aggressive nationalism on the other." Since a great deal of research had already been done on the problem of attitude-formation within the framework of different disciplines, it seemed to me that the most useful initial step to take would be to bring together a small group of experts from different disciplines and different nations to see what they could agree on. Accordingly, I invited eight experts for a two weeks' conference in Paris during the early summer of 1948: Gordon Allport, a psychologist, and Harry Stack Sullivan, a psychiatrist, from the United States; Alexander Szalai, a political scientist, from Hungary; Gilberto Freyre, a sociologist, from Brazil; Dr. John Rickman, a psychoanalyst, from England; Max Horkheimer, a sociologist from Germany; Georges Gurvitch, a sociologist from France; and Arne Naess, a social philosopher from Norway. Otto Klineberg, who was to succeed me as director of the Tensions Project, also participated.

Before these men came, I briefed them carefully on the purposes of the meeting and asked them to prepare in advance a written statement of their position which could serve as a chapter in a book I hoped we could publish after the conference, along with a common statement of points we might agree on. Also before their arrival, I myself drafted what I thought might be a suitable type of "common statement," which we could discuss, revise, and all sign at the end.

It was a memorable conference and a very fruitful one. Most of our time was spent in redrafting the common statement, a process which, of course, involved the airing of each expert's views. This common statement together with the separate contribution of each participant was published in the book, *Tensions that Cause Wars*.[40] An interesting feature of this book, I think, was that each man was invited to comment on the article prepared by his colleagues; and the footnotes of comment, especially those of Szalai, our only Communist participant, make revealing and lively reading.

Another of the resolutions read: "Inquiries into the conceptions which the people of one nation entertain of their own and of other nations." This quite clearly called for reliable survey data on samples of the population in as many countries where survey facilities existed as our budget would permit. So I worked out a draft of the questions I thought would yield a picture of the attitudes people in one nation had towards people in other nations. I then enlisted the help of Alfred Max, Jean Stoetzel, and Hélène Riffault of the French Institute of Public Opinion, and Henry Durant of the British Institute of Public Opinion; met with them for long and pleasant sessions; and eventually had surveys done in Australia, Britain, France, Germany, Italy, The Netherlands, Norway, Mexico, and the United States. I had hoped Dr. Durant would be able to write all this up for us in book form, but the pressure of other duties prevented his doing so. It therefore became necessary for me to have the report written when I returned to Princeton. I was fortunate in obtaining the able help of William Buchanan, then a graduate student of political science at Princeton, who worked part-time with me in the Office of Public Opinion Research. Our analysis appeared in the book, *How Nations See Each Other*.[41]

The findings of the surveys made in the nine different countries showed, among other things, how narrow are the limits of the horizons of most people, how the stereotypes people in one nation have of people in other nations are largely results and not causes of the current relationship of their countries: people in one nation are hostile to people in other nations not because they have unfavorable stereotypes; rather they have these unfavorable stereotypes because they think these other people are interfering with their own or their nation's goals. People in all nations tended to describe their own nationality in highly favorable terms. Respondents who believed that human nature can be changed were more likely than others also to believe it possible for all countries to live together in peace, and those who believed such a peace possible were of course those most favorable to some form of world government.

We suggested actions that might be taken to extend a person's view of the world and bring it into more perspective, such as improving facilities for communication, providing more opportunities by means of which people might get a sense of participation in world affairs, and, above all, creating opportunities that would enable people in different nations to undertake common action for common goals.

19

The Institute for International Social Research

One day in the spring of 1952, Jerry Lambert invited me to have lunch with him and some visiting Princeton classmates. He asked me to bring one of our perception demonstrations. After lunch we went up to Jerry's study and I showed them the rotating trapezoid window described in Chapter 3. I outlined the exciting possibilities of using this approach to understand people in other lands: how research deriving from our transactional point of view might give us a more accurate understanding of the reality worlds of large groups of people.

Jerry's friends, like himself, were all multimillionaires. It was a complete surprise to me when they offered to put up whatever funds might be necessary to try out over a three-year period the subject I had discussed, namely, the possibility of devising studies in countries with distinctly different backgrounds and problems to discover just what assumptions influenced the way people look at themselves and the world around them.

The problem then was to find some way to carry on the

research, for I had a heavy, full-time teaching and administrative load at the University. So I cabled Lloyd Free, who
was then in Rome as Counselor of Embassy and Director of
the United States Information Service in Italy. I had visited
Lloyd a few months earlier and learned that he felt he had
had enough of Government service. Although he was never
in trouble himself, the McCarthy nightmare was at its height
at this time, and he was disgusted that some of his friends
and colleagues were being persecuted while their superiors
did not have the courage to stand up for them. Also, he was
disillusioned because time after time Congress had wrecked
his information program by paring his budget. Congress
was then in the process of cutting back to such a degree that
valuable staff members were being lost, thus wasting all the
money invested in their experience.

Lloyd immediately flew over for a conference with Jerry
and me. He, too, got excited by the possibilities and said he
was willing to take the gamble for three years. This meant
we could proceed at once, for Lloyd was thoroughly familiar
with our transactional view of psychology, had been associated with me in teaching at Princeton as well as in the
various other projects already reported, was skilled in social
research techniques, and is the most sensitive observer I
know.

Within three years Lloyd managed single-handedly to conduct studies of the people in four countries, selected because of differences in their social and political structure and
the varied sociopolitical problems they faced at the time:
Japan, Thailand, Italy, and France.

About 300 copies of each of Lloyd's reports were multi-
lithed and distributed to friends in the academic world and
a number of copies went to various departments and agencies
in the Government. We were gratified to learn that at least
some of them got up to the level of the National Security

Council. In fact, the President's assistant in charge of national security affairs told others that Lloyd's report on Japan was one of the most useful documents the Council had seen during his tenure, indicating as it did the roots and extent of political divergencies in Japan at that time. All four of these studies described the current power and influence structures within the country and showed the contrasting opinions of different interest groups, thus providing realistic bases for policy formation.

In 1955, while Nelson Rockefeller was serving as special assistant to President Eisenhower in charge of problems of psychological warfare, he read Lloyd's reports, knew what we were trying to do, and asked us to come to Washington to talk with him. Nelson had always been a great believer in utilizing psychological concepts and tools for the understanding of peoples. Moreover, he had closely followed the research Del Ames and I had been conducting for some years and was a close friend and admirer of Del's. Nelson wanted to know how we could expand our program. We had to tell him that not only could we not expand it but that we would probably have to give it up entirely. For Lloyd was being offered excellent positions with tenure, and I had more than enough to do to carry on my teaching and administrative duties and to continue with the experimental program, financed by the Rockefeller Foundation, which Ames and I and several younger colleagues were conducting.

Out of the blue, Nelson asked us how much money it would take for Lloyd and me to do what we wanted to do the rest of our lives. Since I had thought he might ask such a question, on the train to Washington I had made a rough calculation that a couple of million dollars, spending both principal and interest, would carry us nicely until retirement age. Nelson's immediate reply was that he would try to get us a million dollars from the Rockefeller Brothers Fund, of which he was then president, and, if he couldn't, he would give us that amount himself. We could start with the million and worry about the rest later.

I thought of Whitehead's statement that "The essence of living is the frustration of established order." [42] I faced a hard decision. I had always loved teaching and Princeton had been very good to me for twenty years. Since I knew I would have to travel a good deal and that we would need various kinds of personnel to help us who would not fit university classifications or salary scales, it would be impossible to combine a university appointment with the vistas opened up by financial independence. But, as in all decisions of the sort, the chief criterion seemed to be: Which is the more challenging course of action? To this there could be only one answer. The generally accepted boundaries of psychology had always rather thwarted me, and a most exciting and irresistible aspect of Nelson's proposal was the chance to spend the rest of my working life trying to push out the dimensions of social psychology, combining experimentation with field studies. The initial endowment of one million dollars was soon forthcoming from the Rockefeller Brothers Fund.

I resigned as Stuart Professor of Psychology and Chairman of the Department of Psychology at Princeton, and Lloyd and I created the nonprofit corporation of the Institute for International Social Research, with Nelson as one of our distinguished trustees. I might say, parenthetically, that the kind of situation I was in, the dream of anyone interested in basic research, imposes a haunting sense of responsibility, since no one really cares what you do except yourself and you keep wondering if you are doing your best.

This is not the place to review all the research done by Lloyd and me under the aegis of the Institute. Much of my own energy has been devoted to a search for a more systematic and factual understanding of what propels people to behave as they do and to acquire the perceptions and attitudes they have; also how they can learn to act in ways that will better achieve both their own purposes and those of their fellow-men. Central to the search is our basic transactional psychological approach. I have always had in my Princeton office a set of the Ames demonstrations in perception to show our colleagues and many visitors just how the field work, so much of it done by Lloyd, ties in with the nature of man's perception and his construction of his own unique reality world.

20

A Way to Reach the Russian People

Late in 1957, after completing the study of protest voters in France and Italy, I became increasingly interested in extending my perception research to what appeared to me an important area: how do Soviet leaders perceive human nature? The first reason for my interest in this question was the desire to find out if the studies on perceptual processes that Ames and I, along with younger colleagues, had been conducting for a decade would increase our understanding of Soviet leaders; second, I wanted to see if any of our conclusions could be translated into practical suggestions for President Eisenhower to use, particularly if he had an opportunity himself to visit the Soviet Union and give television talks to the Soviet people. There was a good deal of speculation at the time about the possibility of such a trip. A few years later a visit was actually planned, but the invitation was withdrawn by Premier Nikita Khrushchev in Paris when he refused to participate in the Summit Conference scheduled to meet there on May 16, 1960, and demanded, instead, an apology from Eisenhower for the flight over the Soviet Union by a United States U-2 reconnaissance plane, which the Soviets had shot down on May 1.

The methods of research and the conclusions reached concerning the views of human nature which Soviet leaders had at the time were published in 1960 in a book entitled *Soviet Leaders and Mastery Over Man.*[43] An additional reason for the study was to try to find out what was going on in Soviet psychology, what psychologists in the Soviet Union were being allowed to study. I invited two other psychologists to take the trip with me, Professor Henry A. Murray of Harvard and Professor Mark May of Yale. I also took with me Professor Fred Barghoorn of Yale and Mr. Melville Ruggles, two experts in Soviet politics who knew the country as well as the language.[44] Our visit to the Soviet Union was in November and early December of 1958.

Shortly after my return, I prepared an informal memorandum of suggestions about United States policy vis-à-vis the Soviet Union for General Andrew Goodpaster, White House staff secretary, to pass on to President Eisenhower if he saw fit. The memorandum, dated January 3, 1959, was based not only on the impressions gained during our trip but on other data I had by that time assembled. Excerpts from this memorandum follow:

> The official position of the United States Government toward the Soviet regime must, I agree, remain firm. At the same time, however, there do seem to be opportunities to reach the Soviet people themselves on the level of human values, thus transcending their ideological preconceptions.
>
> Because the Soviet State is now viable and non-revolutionary and because the people are proud of its world position as a nation and attribute its increase in world stature to Socialism or Communism (the words are used interchangeably), we might do well to omit from all news and information addressed to the Russian people any

statements or terms that would appear derogatory to them, such as the word "Reds."

We should avoid any talk about ideology and simply describe what we are doing, what we are thinking, how the United States is providing more security and more opportunity for people to develop themselves. In brief, we should do everything possible to demonstrate the effectiveness of our system.

We should take every opportunity to give the Soviet people as many models as we can, whether of a material or nonmaterial nature, of a sort they will be able to copy or adapt sooner or later. It is, of course, of the utmost importance to select only models that are practicable and possible for the Soviet people to imitate and to lead them step by step to more advanced levels of imitation. Once they see something that has already proved useful and satisfying to people elsewhere, they will have a springboard from which to take off on their own. A trivial but glaring example is their enormous interest in American jazz, with all its emphasis on self-expression. If our conversations with psychologists and social scientists provide any indication, people are eager to break through stereotypes in many fields.

Because of the pride of Soviet citizens in what has been achieved, because of their sense of inferiority, and because of their frank admission that they want to be more like us, it would appear that we should take a more positive approach to their achievements, such as congratulating the people on any clearly progressive step they make. They seem to crave security and appreciation from us. While we obviously cannot promise security as long as their regime is a threat to our own security, we should benefit in the long run by showing them our appreciation and approval whenever we can. The President's congratulation on the first Sputnik provides an excellent precedent. This can be done in the context of our democratic values. We have a real opportunity, I believe, gradually to bring Soviet achievements and expectancies more in line with our own, thus slowly helping to overcome the separation of the Soviet State from the Soviet people and allowing the sincere desire of the people for peace and a higher standard of living to counteract any designs of the regime for world domination.

Without indulging in ideological discussion, we might emphasize in various contexts that Soviet leaders are thwarting the creative talents of the people in literature, the arts, the social sciences, production, and the like by their narrow interpretation of Marx and Lenin.

Instead of ridiculing and criticizing elections in the Soviet Union or other Communist countries, we might take them as opportunities to point out that large majority votes for a single party are naturally interpreted by everyone in the non-Communist world as basic signs of weakness, not of strength, and express our hope that the citizens of Communist countries will be able to have a stronger voice in their governments.

We might try to adopt the Soviet and Nazi strategy of spoiling or confusing the meaning of certain key propaganda terms. While the following could obviously not be used because of domestic political considerations, it is an example of what I mean: describe our own economic system as *socialistic Capitalism* and theirs as *capitalistic Socialism,* thus implying that their system is not the only one concerned with the welfare of the people and hence that the survival of their system does not depend on the destruction of ours.

In spite of the present need for firm policies with respect to the Soviet regime, the United States could, I believe, win a great moral victory with favorable repercussions in many areas of the world if, at the right moments, we could find dramatic and imaginative ways to demonstrate that we are strong enough, confident enough, and big enough to be beyond pride and the need to save face.

Many people throughout the world clearly regard the United States and the Soviet Union as they would two bull moose who have locked horns or two men who have to fight a duel: the tragedy of pride. The right, well-conceived action at the right time could convey an impression of our humility and idealism in contrast to the arrogance and self-righteousness of the Soviet regime and would be bound to win friends and be taken as a sign of sincerity and strength.

General Goodpaster called a few days later to ask if I would come down and have lunch with the President, who had liked the memorandum, said it had given him some ideas, and wanted to talk with me. General Goodpaster and the President's son, John, were the only others at the luncheon, which lasted about two hours. I elaborated on the points made in the memorandum and minced no words about how far off the beam I thought Secretary of State John Foster Dulles was in many of his remarks, citing a statement he had made only the day before in which he called the Soviets "stupid."

One of the problems on the President's mind was the immediately forthcoming visit of Mr. Anastas Mikoyan. The President cited someone's comment that Mr. Mikoyan was as shrewd as all the Armenian rug merchants wrapped up into one rug and also cited Dulles's remark that if you didn't know Mikoyan was a man, you would fall in love with him. I suggested that the President use Mikoyan's visit as an opportunity to get a message to the Soviet people by sending a telegram to him just before his return to the Soviet Union from America. The President liked the idea and said perhaps anything should be tried, for things couldn't be worse than they were at the time. I said I would prepare my thoughts for such a message and did so after lunch on a typewriter in the basement of the White House. I was particularly eager to have the President describe the Soviet system as state capitalism.

I sensed during the luncheon that the President liked the type of recommendations I was making chiefly because they confirmed his own instincts, instincts he was often not able to follow because of pressures put on him by Dulles and others. At a luncheon in the White House a few weeks later, attended by a large number of people to discuss the forthcoming United States exhibit for the Moscow Fair, the President walked over to me with a big grin on his face and asked if I had seen Mikoyan's reply to the telegram sent to him by Dulles.

My suggestions to the President for his message to Mikoyan included the usual expression of appreciation for his visit, the desire of our Government and people for peace, our wish that there could be more visits and exchanges, etc. The particular thought I wanted to inject was that Mr. Mikoyan had had an opportunity to see the progress we are making under our system of individual capitalism just as we are seeing the progress his country is making under its system of state capitalism.

The message sent by Secretary Dulles said:

> As you leave the United States, please allow me, on behalf of the President, myself, and other officials you have met, to express our personal hope that your visit has been of value and that you will convey to the people

of the Soviet Union an expression of the sincere desire of the people of the United States for friendship with them.

Through your visit we hope that you can report to Premier Khrushchev that you have gained an understanding of the attitudes of our people—not only of the desire for peace that they and their government share so deeply with people everywhere, but also of their unswerving belief, irrespective of their political party, in the right of people to determine their own form of government.

You know President Eisenhower's feeling that more visits and exchanges can help us to understand each other and assist the people of both countries basically to share the goals of security, ever-improving standards of living, and ever-increasing opportunities for personal development. The President is aware that you operate under a system of state capitalism, and he hopes it has been useful to you to have seen the progress of our people under our system of individual capitalism. We are sure that you have found the experience interesting.

For both peoples, the President expresses hope for advancement of that enduring spirit of peace and friendship which must bring benefit to the people themselves.

The next day Mikoyan, while en route home, replied to the telegram he had received. The *New York Times* reported on January 23, 1959:

Anastas I. Mikoyan told Secretary of State Dulles in a telegram today that the United States and Soviet Governments were obligated to end the "cold war" and establish good-neighbor relations as soon as possible.

The communication from Mr. Mikoyan, a Soviet First Deputy Premier, was sent from Argentia, Newfoundland, where his plane made an emergency landing because of engine trouble. It was in reply to a farewell telegram from Mr. Dulles delivered aboard the plane. . . .

Mr. Mikoyan said his trip across the United States had confirmed him in the conviction that the people of the United States, like that of the Soviet Union, would like to see an end of the propaganda war between their Governments. He added: "It is the great responsibility of both our Governments to see that these desires are fulfilled as soon as possible."

The Soviet official made no specific suggestion on how to end the "cold war." "As you know," Mr. Mikoyan said in his letter, "I have tried to express in my talks with President Eisenhower, yourself and other American statesmen, and also in my conversations with representatives of various groups of the American population, our desire to have the 'cold war' ended and security guaranteed for the peoples of the world under conditions of peaceful co-existence."

The Soviet leader went on to suggest that the fact that the United States was a capitalist country and the Soviet Union "a Socialist country building communism" should not interfere with the cooperation of both "in the interests of strengthening peace."

Secretary Dulles had referred to the Soviet system in his telegram as "state capitalism" as distinguished from the "individual capitalism" of the American way. Mr. Mikoyan said Mr. Dulles had used "a strange definition of the Soviet system."

The day after President Eisenhower returned from the ill-fated Paris conference, May 21, 1960, I forwarded to him through General Goodpaster some recommendations relating to United States information themes concerned with the Soviet Union. The memorandum contained the preliminary note: "While these recommendations may not be new and may have been heard before, if they have any validity, it is essential that they be repeated often in rifle shot fashion." The memorandum elaborated the following points:

We should try to pound home to people everywhere, especially those in neutral areas, the fact that the Communist Party uses nations and states and the people who compose them as instruments or tools to carry out Party policies. In other words, the Party comes first and is regarded as everlasting, while nations or states and their people are secondary.

We should make clear that the issue dividing people is not Communism or Socialism versus Capitalism but the dictatorship of the Communist Party versus democracy. To people in the underdeveloped areas, we should emphasize that the only real enemy of strong national leaders is the Communist Party.

We should indicate that while Soviet leaders talk about coexistence, in reality they seem to be afraid of it. They do not like their people to know too much about democracy; they restrict both information and travel.

We should be able to out-compete the Soviet Union in teaching people in underdeveloped areas what to want, how to seek real progress and civilization; we should show that an open society can offer not only higher standards of living and security but a whole range and quality of satisfactions impossible in a state where freedom and choice are restricted.

We should counteract the Soviet strategy of minimizing the similarities and maximizing the differences between modern industrial states. They have many problems in common and are likely to have more.

We should compliment the Soviet people on the advances they have made in their standard of living and on gaining somewhat more freedom of action as a result of their hardships and sacrifices.

We should intensify and expand all forms of exchanges, since there seems little doubt that we have much more to gain from these in terms of influencing Soviet people than Soviet leaders have to gain by any influence on us. Dramatic proposals for exchanges of all kinds, which we would expect Soviet leaders to reject, might bring their censorship, controls, and fear of comparison into bolder relief.

As soon as the news of Vice President Nixon's intended visit to the Soviet Union was announced, I wrote General Goodpaster on April 17, 1959, that there were a number of salient reasons why I thought it would be a good idea if Mrs. Nixon accompanied the Vice President to Moscow. Among these reasons was the fact that the Soviet people would be somewhat startled and pleased for a high official to bring his wife along and that the curiosity and interest of Soviet women would be particularly aroused by Mrs. Nixon's presence. For in spite of the fact that women are in Soviet theory on a par with men, the operational fact is that women are very often excluded from many Soviet social affairs. Mr. Nixon wrote on May 4, 1959, thanking me for the suggestion and saying Mrs. Nixon would accompany him on the trip.

21

Human Concerns

In this chapter I report very briefly on a research project undertaken with the aim of finding out on a wider scope and with greater depth than I ever had before the things that this book has been concerned with throughout. Although the results of this research have been published in detail, I include a sketch of some of them here to illustrate the sort of social science research with policy implications that is possible for two people to do with relatively modest funds.[45]

Together, Lloyd Free and I managed to have sample populations interviewed on the same questions in fourteen different countries representing approximately 30 per cent of the world's population. The countries included in the study were Brazil, Cuba, the Dominican Republic, Egypt, India, Israel, Japan, Nigeria, Panama, the Philippines, Poland, the United States, West Germany, and Yugoslavia. The total sample of people was over 20,000 cases. Lloyd and I traveled more than 250,000 miles to organize and supervise the work, often making three visits to a country to see that the research was properly and carefully done. This study winds up a phase of the work of our Institute for International Social Research that took eight years, from 1957 to

1965, to complete. All the research was financed from the endowment given the Institute by the Rockefeller Brothers Fund.

In order to learn in a person's own terms and from his own point of view what his concerns are and how he feels he stands in relation to where he would like to be in life, we employ a device called the Self-Anchoring Striving Scale invented for our purposes, the same scale as that described in Chapters 1 and 2. By means of this method we learn, in a person's own words and his own terms and without our superimposing any categories or ideas for him to respond to, just what his hopes and aspirations, his fears and worries are for himself and his country. In order to compare individuals and groups of individuals either within nations or between nations, Lloyd and I very carefully worked out a coding scheme that could handle nearly all responses given by any people anywhere in the world. This also enables us to relate the concerns of people to the position they give themselves and their nation on the ladder of life in the present, past, and future.

Only a few illustrative results will be mentioned here. Each provides information that responsible policy makers might well take into account in plans dealing with economic aid, effective communication, international cooperation, and the like.

It is abundantly clear from these studies that at the present stage of human and societal development, the vast majority of people's hopes and fears revolve around the complex of personal well-being as this is rather simply and genuinely defined: a decent standard of living; opportunities for children; technological advances; good health; a good job; decent housing; a happy home life; better educational facilities. Relatively few hopes take on a more idealistic or sophisticated character, although an improved sense of social and political responsibility, of being useful to others, and the aspiration for self-development are mentioned by at least 5 per cent of the total population sampled. But concern for greater social justice, more freedom, better moral standards, the resolution of moral or ethical problems and similar goals appears to be the conscious concern of only a tiny minority of people throughout the world. Similarly, with a few exceptions, there is little concern for ideology as this term is commonly used: few people are basically interested in concepts such as democracy, socialism, communism, or capitalism as such, and in none of the nations studied, including the two Communist countries of Poland and Yugoslavia, do the people seem the least bit interested in aggressively extending to others the ideology under which their state operates.

There are wide variations in the total volume and range of the hopes and fears people in different countries express both for themselves and for their nations and, of course, great differences in the range of hopes mentioned by educated people and people living in cities as compared with the range of hopes of less educated people and those in rural areas. It is clear that people must learn what to want the way they learn anything else; they must learn the range and quality of experience that should be theirs if things are to be different. Among the people of India, for example, less than 10 per cent are worried about their health while in health-conscious America and West Germany this figure rises to 40 per cent.

The outstanding worry people in the total sample have for their country is that it might become involved in another war. But it is noteworthy that among people who have not recently experienced the ravages of war, such as the Nigerians and Brazilians, the fear of war is mentioned by only a small minority; whereas in the case of people who lived through the horrors of war, such as the Poles, the Yugoslavs, and the

West Germans, the overwhelming majority account the fear of war the major fear for their country.

Large differences are found in the way people rate themselves on the ladder of life with respect to where they feel they stand now, where they were five years ago, and where they think they will be five years in the future. The lowest rating found for the present was among the Dominicans, whose average rating on the scale was 1.6; the highest rating for the present was among Americans with their average of 6.6. The standards and expectations by means of which people judge their own progress are of course relative to their own experience: people in less developed countries have not yet learned all that is potentially available, and their needs are modest indeed compared with those of people living in advanced societies.

Nearly everyone felt himself better off at the time of our studies than he had been in the past, except for most people in the Dominican Republic and the Philippines. And all people without exception expect significant improvement in the future both for themselves and for their nations, a fact that leads to the observation that hope seems to be universal and indeed to spring eternal. The greatest overall shifts upwards in the ladder ratings occurred among people whose countries had recently been established or achieved independence, such as Cuba, the Dominican Republic, Nigeria, Egypt, Yugoslavia, and Israel. The ratings given both their own and their nation's future by people in underdeveloped countries were rather extravagant, implying both a relative lack of knowledge of the high quality and wide range of standards possible and an ignorance or underestimation of the many difficulties ahead before what aspirations they have can be realized. These ratings together with other data underscore the force of nationalism and national pride in today's world, a force no policy maker must ever lose sight of.

The findings in the study point to stages of psychological development that seem to characterize large numbers of people in the modern nation-state. The following five phases of such development can be differentiated: for example— (1) the acquiescence to circumstances characteristic of so many Indians and Brazilians; (2) an awakening consciousness of the possibilities of increasing the range or quality of satisfactions characteristic of many Yugoslav peasants, and of Filipinos in the lower socio-economic bracket; (3) the awareness that the new potentialities can be realized, a phase that seems to characterize Nigerians, for one; (4) the assurance and self-reliance derived from achieving the goals desired, a phase that Israel seems to be in; and, finally, (5) the satisfaction Americans show with a way of life that promises continuing development.

In concluding the study I noted that every social and political system can be regarded as an experiment in the broad perspective of time and that, whatever the circumstances, the human design will in the long run force any institutional framework to accommodate it. Obviously if the expectations of people in a number of the countries studied and others throughout the world are not supported by the drastic reforms required to bring about a sense of improvement, then serious trouble may be expected.

22

The Psychological Dimensions of Policy

During the last two decades the United States has become the dominant military and economic power of the world. The problems of formulating and articulating its foreign policy have necessarily become more complex as United States power, expressed through its foreign policy, makes ever greater impact upon the policies of other nations throughout the world. The greater the impact of power the greater the reaction to it, whether in the form of fear or envy or admiration.

It has been the burden of this book that it is possible for the United States to determine to a far greater extent than has been realized, either by our government or our social scientists, which form this reaction takes. Moreover, that we can largely determine the kind of reaction by means of the psychological tools I have described.

Unfortunately, these tools are barely known to those who make and articulate policy. I once briefly thought I had the opportunity to persuade President Kennedy to make effective use of them on at least one front. On December 9, 1960, I got an unexpected telephone call. It was from John Sharon, who graduated from Princeton in 1949 and had been one of the ablest undergraduates it was my pleasure to teach. After college and law school, John had been closely associated with Adlai Stevenson in his two presidential campaigns. Through his association with Stevenson, John became known to President-elect Kennedy, who was now asking John and his senior law partner, George Ball (later Undersecretary of State), if they would organize certain task forces charged with preparing memoranda to assist him in thinking about many of the urgent problems he would face after his inauguration. One of the subjects John and George Ball were asked to survey through a special task force was the Government's whole information program abroad. John was calling me to consult about what should be done to get the project started at once.

My reply was to suggest Lloyd Free as the best man in the country to head up this particular survey. Lloyd shared with me a long-standing, deep concern about the effectiveness of our whole information program. We were agreed that radical steps were necessary to make it effective, and Lloyd had a wide background of experience, both in Washington as one-time Acting Director of International Information in the Department of State, and also in the field, where he had served as Counsellor of Embassy for Public Affairs in Italy and had done a great deal of research on the political dynamics of people in many countries. Furthermore, Lloyd was living in Washington and could easily get in touch with the many people there whose views ought to be solicited.

Both John and Lloyd concurred with this suggestion and Lloyd and I met with John in his Washington office three days later, on December 12. A report on the survey had to be in the hands of the President-elect in less than three weeks. I prepared a paper for Lloyd in which I set forth my ideas. The aid of W. Phillips Davison, a close friend of Lloyd's, who had been a student of mine and later had succeeded Lloyd as Editor of the *Public Opinion Quarterly*, was also conscripted, and Lloyd and Phill then quickly organized a task force. I was one of about a dozen members of the group. Lloyd and Phill put in long days and nights soliciting the views of the various members appointed to the task force. By the first of January 1961, a memorandum spelling out specifically and in detail the problems of government information policy, together with many recommendations—ranging all the way from organization to theory and operations—was in President-elect Kennedy's hands. Since the document was confidential, its contents cannot be revealed here. Both Lloyd and I received letters from President Kennedy thanking us for our work.

Edward R. Murrow, who had been a member of the task force and was subsequently named Director of USIA, was fond of saying that the task force report was his Bible, and President Kennedy, in his letter to me dated June 7, 1961, spoke of the report as "of continuing use to me and my Administration." Yet neither Lloyd nor I was ever able to detect that the major recommendations of the report were implemented to the slightest degree. Those sections bearing on the overall theory of what an information program should be and what reorganization and restructuring were required to effectuate policy were never echoed in any official action in later months and years.

This disillusioning, frustrating, and disappointing experience illustrates the tragic underestimation of the importance of a whole area of operation that the United States Government neglects at its peril and at extreme detriment to its formulation and conduct of effective foreign policy. How, if this were not so, could recommendations for such a crucial aspect of government have been assigned to an *ad hoc* task force on a crash-program basis? And how could the two men most responsible for implementing such recommendations—the President and his director of information—assert the recommendations had been taken seriously when later performance proved they had not?

The truth is that the essential problem has not been understood. It may sound simple-minded to say that a whole new way of thinking must be introduced into policy planning, into the very expression of policy at all levels of government, and into all important governmental communication, but this is the major conclusion I have reached after twenty years of active experimentation and anxious concern. This new way of thinking entails more than a mere intellectual process: it entails a new way of feeling, a genuine empathic, imaginative understanding of the people the policy is designed to affect. When we meet someone we know we ask him, "How are you?" "Wie geht's?" "Comment ça va?" according to the language we have learned. And, depending on the genuineness of the interest, a genuine response can generally be got without much trouble.

But we need to extend our concern for the feelings of people far beyond the boundaries of our own family, circle of friends, community, nation, and race. Until we take into account the feelings of other people—whether they happen to live in Vietnam, the Soviet Union, China, Israel, India, Nigeria, or any other spot on the globe—American foreign policy will be lacking in the most important of all human dimensions.

This new way of thinking would first of all discard the defensive, cold-war stance of American foreign policy ever since the end of World War II. In spite of all the agencies, bureaus, and committees ostensibly set up to plan and develop stable, viable policy, our planning, diplomatic actions, and information dissemination in these postwar years have been characterized by short-range, day-to-day reactions to international crises. Such reflexive responses are hopelessly inadequate and futile. No merchandiser could stay in business if he allowed himself to be put on the defensive, contenting himself with repeated explanations of why his product is not as bad as his competitors say it is. By the same token, no government can hope to get its policies understood and accepted by spending its time and energy answering incessant attacks.

Second, the new way of thinking would involve relating our foreign policy to the revolution of rising expectations now sweeping the whole world. It would deter us from supporting any regime that seeks merely to preserve the status quo, even on just a local front, and that refuses to work for progressive economic, social, and cultural changes.

Third, it would take fully into account the force, the blessing, and the curse of nationalism, including neutral nationalism. For at this period of history and until nationalism runs its course, the concept of nationalism is the rallying point for an increasing number of people. This fact has been overlooked in the ceaseless efforts to make other countries help the United States counteract Communism. Policy positions and actions guided *only* by anti-Communism obscure much more fundamental problems, among them the conditions that give rise to Communism. And, incidentally, there should be no more talk about "psychological warfare": the term should be dropped from both official thinking and official vocabularies. It is of no use in constructing imaginative, coordinated diplomacy.

Now, if it is not already too late, is the time for a bold, imaginative, effective foreign policy and overseas information program commensurate with United States power and consonant with its long-range purposes. The indispensable first step in creating foreign policy is, of course, the charting of long-range objectives, as is now done by the President, the Department of State, the National Security Council, and others. These officials and agencies determine such broad goals as those set up for the Alliance for Progress in Latin America; assisting the developing nations to achieve a measure of economic improvement and self-sufficiency and to establish viable democracies; influencing the nations of Western and Eastern Europe in a direction that will bring about closer cooperation among them and with us; constantly seeking agreements with the Soviet Union to our mutual advantage and in furtherance of peace; preventing the exploitation of people in small, weak nations or their take-over by Communists or other authoritarian groups. All such goals are clearly in our national and personal interests, all are extensions of the basic principles of our democratic tradition.

Even though the formulation of basic substantive goals is clearly the responsibility of the high government officials involved, under certain circumstances it may be difficult for them to know just what policies should be followed. Information may be lacking in specific situations concerning the feasibility of alternative policies or their compatibility with long-range objectives because of ignorance of the aspirations, concerns, loyalties, and beliefs of the people involved and the leadership available. In such instances policy research could be crucial in the formulation of substantive goals themselves.

The equally indispensable second step is to translate these long-range policy aims into the psychological objectives necessary to attain them. For example, in furthering the Alliance for Progress, we ought to know the extent to which the people in the countries involved are receptive or resistant to change; the degree to which they are able to see that programs of the Alliance for Progress are related to the improvement of their own standards of living. We should study the sensitivity and value-structure of the élite governing groups to find out whether or not they are sincerely motivated to undertake developments in line with United States objectives and whether or not they are democratically oriented.

An effective psychological approach also requires an understanding of the awareness or ignorance of the American people themselves about long-range objectives as well as knowledge of their concern with and interest in these objectives. No matter how difficult this aspect of the job may appear to be, there is no way out of it in a democratic government based on a presumably enlightened electorate, which must understand and care before it can choose, support, or criticize wisely. The American people are quick to spot any approach that is purely defensive and that goes against their own and their nation's best interests once they understand the issues involved.

The formulation of psychological objectives, with the aid of highly relevant research, is required to anticipate probable reactions and resistances to various contingencies that may be foreseen and to various means of attaining goals. There is no reason in this day and age of increasingly sophisticated research techniques for policy to be devised quite so much by guess-work and hunch. Moreover, translation of long-range objectives into psychological objectives as an intervening step to action would increase the effectiveness of economic, military, informational, cultural, and all other United States efforts.

But this formulation of psychological objectives and the translation of them into manageable, realistic programs for effective communication to specific groups cannot be left to busy men who are saddled with the day-to-day responsibilities of administering various departments and agencies of the Government. They would probably be the first to agree that it is impossible within the present framework for them to have the freedom required to devise long-range, systematic programs. They are involved in endless staff meetings where ideas and proposals are edited to death; they are faced with deadlines; they have limited budgets; they get involved in the petty jealousies of inter-agency and interdepartmental rivalries and power struggles; their responsibilities are limited, sometimes not clear; their efforts are scattered. It is little wonder that the whole Government effort to communicate effectively with people all over the world is characterized by a pedestrian, routine, thoroughly inadequate, and unimaginative approach. At the same time, under the circumstances that now prevail, it is remarkable that the many dedicated people involved in policy formulation and communication do as well as they do.

In my diary for July 22, 1942, when I was intimately involved in the Washington scene, I find the following entry: "The whole situation with respect to information and intelligence has made me feel blue all week. It is as though one's mother had been taken to the hospital for a serious operation where, instead of having a few good surgeons work on her, one had all the freshmen in a medical school class doing little bits of the operation in a very inexperienced, amateurish way." Now, over two decades later, I unfortunately seek in vain for reasons to alter that judgment when I look at the current scene.

What can be done to overcome this state of affairs?

The first step, I believe, is to set up on an adequate scale the machinery for securing as accurate an appraisal as possible of the state of mind of people with whom we are trying to communicate. By the state of mind of a people, I mean, above all, their feelings, the whole complex of their hopes and aspirations, their frustrations and fears, the way all these, together with traditions and customs, determine how people look at themselves and the world. For it has become crystal clear that the way people perceive things is in large part fashioned by the assumptions they bring to situations. I have called this a person's "assumptive world" or his "reality world." Each of us has his own reality world, sharing many aspects of it with others like us. It is the only world we know. For each of us, our own psychological world is just as real as sticks and stones, money, food, or guns. No matter how the reality worlds of others may differ from our own, it is imperative that we try not only to understand them but to respect them. This is the only course of intelligent, decent behavior. The problem has been nicely put by George Kennan: "The sources of tragedy in international life lie in the differences of outlook that divide the human race; and it seems to me that our purposes prosper only when something happens in the mind of another person, and perhaps in our own mind as well, which makes it easier for all of us to see each other's problems and prejudices with detachment and to live peaceably side by side." [46] Various studies reported in this volume attest to the consequences to the United States when it failed to take these factors into account.

If policy planners, from the President on down, through cabinet officers, department heads, agency directors, Congressmen, ambassadors, commanders of the armed forces, and all others in any way involved in formulating policies and policy statements, fail to consider the psychological context provided by people's reality worlds, then effective, penetrating, honest, humanitarian communication becomes impossible. The policy planners will continue to flounder, to rely solely on military or economic power or on old-line diplomacy to attain policy objectives. They will thus unnecessarily poison the atmosphere in which they must operate and, perhaps, conclude out of sheer frustration that the people they are trying to deal with are unresponsive, ungrateful, or short-sighted.

The second step necessary to establish a psychologically

intelligent policy is to provide the proper machinery for close, systematic coordination of psycho-political research and policy planning and execution. Perhaps the reader has assumed that this existed all along. But, in fact, there simply is no adequate psycho-political research going on that is planned far enough ahead either to help develop policy or to devise and utilize the most effective modes of communication.

Even if pertinent research has been done either by private or Governmental organizations, those entrusted with policy decisions are all too often quite unaware of it. Reports get buried in bureaucratic files. Communication between policy planners and research people is a relatively hit-and-miss affair. Both the planners and the researchers are often quite unaware of the real potentialities of psycho-political research, and the researchers, if they are aware, are usually left out of the early phases of planning and are unable to start work even if they have the funds and facilities. Practically no psycho-political research undertaken in the academic community is of the type a policy planner would find immediately useful, and practically none of it is accompanied by political judgment. It is, then, by no means the fault of responsible policy planners alone that research tends to be neglected: psychologists and social scientists themselves have sadly neglected this whole field.

A coordinated research and policy program would not only delineate and focus the urgencies and priorities of domestic concerns, frustrations, and allegiances in the nations with which the United States is dealing. It would also produce a genuine knowledge of the real structure of power and influence in those nations, and thus be able to identify the groups most likely to be influential in promoting United States policy, whether this concerns specific phases of economic, social, military, or cultural objectives. In practice the power structure may be quite different from what it is in theory or on organization charts. Once these groups are identified and differentiated from one another, then research can help determine effective ways to communicate with them, in order to achieve policy objectives without embarrassing or contravening normal channels of diplomacy by such naive and heavy-handed research efforts as have sometimes been made.

Pilot studies would enable the information operation to use a "rifle shot" approach, consistently directed at known targets, rather than a "shot gun" approach, based on the theory that if we scatter ammunition widely enough we may hit something. Furthermore, continued research can determine whether or not the approaches used are having the desired effect and, if not, help to devise better alternatives.

The objective of the new approach proposed here goes far beyond current official "information" objectives. Portraying a "full and fair picture of America" or "telling the truth about America" are not really ultimate goals. Of course we want to tell the truth and present a fair picture. But these oversimplifications provide no operating guides whatever. Such conceptions hamstring many of our information programs. Worse, they overlook the basic fact that the purpose of efforts to explain policy, or provide information, or export cultural programs is to further the substantive objectives and policies of the United States. There is no necessary correlation between presenting this "full and fair picture," or simply "telling the truth," and the furtherance of such objectives and policies.

Americans want to feel that they are popular just as other people do. But it is not so easy for them to be popular because they are regarded by most people in other parts of the world as rich. Confucius once said, "I never gave you anything so why do you hate me?" Yet basically whether or not the

people of a country "like" America has no necessary relation to actions they take either in domestic or foreign areas.
The research of our own Institute and many of the surveys publicly reported by the United States Information
Agency continuously reveal the popularity of the United
States among nearly all other peoples, a popularity infinitely greater than that of the Soviet Union. But the popularity of America in Italy, for example, does not keep a sizable
proportion of Italians from voting Communist; the popularity of America in India does not affect Indian neutralism.
The people in Italy and India, as in other parts of the world,
vote on issues that are important *to them* as *they* themselves
see them and what they think of the United States is, to
them, completely irrelevant to most of these issues.

Most people in most parts of the world care little about
ideologies, either Communist or democratic. People want a
higher standard of living, they want progress, they want the
benefits of civilization and technology. To the extent that
policy and news dissemination remain on the defensive, the
United States loses a tremendous opportunity to help teach
people what progress, civilization, and democracy can mean.
In other words, the proposal I am making would involve
the crucial job of helping people everywhere learn what to
want, what the standards are by means of which "progress," "civilization," and "democracy" are to be defined and
judged. Incidentally, the United States need not fear Communist competition in this regard, since the Communist
definition of such terms is relatively so restricted and since
its use of people for its self-interested aims sooner or later
becomes patently clear.

On balance, perhaps no great power in history has a better
record than Americans for extending a helping hand, especially since World War II. But to the recipient it is often
not so much what you give as how you give it. And without

long-range policies supported by a thorough awareness—on the part of government, communications, and electorate—of the full psychological dimension, we cannot obtain our basic humanitarian objectives. We must begin with education, for there are few trained and sensitive people prepared to deal with the problem of introducing the full psychological dimension into policy formation. There is really no place where people are being trained in the way of thinking I am urging here.

I submit that the undertaking is possible.* The stakes are enormous, infinitely higher than most people realize. Continued neglect of the psychological problems involved in the formulation of particular foreign policy objectives and in effective international relations and communications means continual multiplication of the chances of failure or near-failure. And such failures and near-failures, we know from repeated experiences in the past, cost lives and substance. Furthermore, such neglect means lessening the prestige of, respect for, and confidence in the United States and impairs the country's role as a leader of the free world.

* I have indicated my own thought as to how psychological dimensions might be geared into foreign policy considerations in Note 47 (pp. 190–193) at the end of this volume.

Notes

1. This account is taken from the complete study written by Lloyd A. Free, *Attitudes of the Cuban People toward the Castro Regime* (Princeton, N.J.: Institute for International Social Research, July 1960).

2. The device used in this research is called The Self-Anchoring Striving Scale and is described in detail in my book, *The Pattern of Human Concerns* (New Brunswick, N.J.: Rutgers University Press, 1965).

3. Lloyd A. Free, *The Attitudes, Hopes and Fears of the Dominican People* (Princeton, N.J.: Institute for International Social Research, 1962, 1965).

4. The following publications describe in detail the theoretical basis of the research reported here: Hadley Cantril, *The Psychology of Social Movements* (New York: Wiley, 1941; paperback edition, 1963); Hadley Cantril, *The "Why" of Man's Experience* (New York: Macmillan, 1950); Hadley Cantril, *The Politics of Despair* (New York: Basic Books, 1958; paperback edition, New York: Collier, 1962), Chapter 1, on "The Nature of Our Reality Worlds"; Hadley Cantril, *The Pattern of Human Concerns* (New Brunswick, N.J.: Rutgers University Press, 1965), Chapters 1, 2, 16. For a description of the perception demonstrations, see William Ittelson, *The Ames Demonstrations in Perception* (Princeton University Press, 1952). For reports of a number of experiments utilizing the perception demonstrations, see F. P. Kilpatrick, *Explorations in Transactional Psychology* (New

York University Press, 1961). Illustrations from literature reflecting the transactional view are contained in Hadley Cantril and Charles H. Bumstead, *Reflections on the Human Venture* (New York University Press, 1960). The thinking of Adelbert Ames, Jr., is found in *The Morning Notes of Adelbert Ames, Jr.,* ed. Hadley Cantril (New Brunswick, N.J.: Rutgers University Press, 1960). A detailed account of the theory and construction of the rotating trapezoid window will be found in Adelbert Ames, Jr., "Visual Perception and the Rotating Trapezoidal Window," *Psychological Monographs,* 1951, No. 324. The neurophysiological processes involved in psychological transactions are discussed in Hadley Cantril and William K. Livingston, "The Concept of Transaction in Psychology and Neurology," *Journal of Individual Psychology,* 1963, vol. 19, pp. 3–16.

5. Hadley Cantril, "The Social Psychology of Everyday Life," *Psychological Bulletin,* 1934, pp. 297–330.

6. Prior to the election of 1936, the *Literary Digest,* a weekly news magazine, launched another of its "polls," largely as a publicity stunt. It attracted enormous interest. The editors of the *Literary Digest* sent out over 10,000,000 ballots by mail; of these 2,350,176 were returned and duly tabulated. The *Literary Digest* predicted that Roosevelt would obtain 40.9 per cent of the votes and, of course, lose the election. The actual vote for Roosevelt in 1936 was 60.7 per cent. While the *Literary Digest* with its huge number of cases had an error of 19.8 per cent, the "scientific" polls at the time all predicted Roosevelt's victory: both the Gallup and Crossley polls gave him 53.8 per cent while the *Fortune* poll gave him 61.7 per cent. The average deviation of the Gallup poll from final election returns in fifteen national elections is 2.9 percentage points; this is reduced to 1.9 percentage points for the eight national elections held since 1948 when probability sampling was used.

The reason for the debacle of the *Literary Digest* was that it failed completely to get any true sampling of the population, depending as it did on sending its ballots by mail to readily available sources, such as people listed in telephone books or on automobile registration lists. It was therefore heavily weighted toward the upper income, Republican population. A detailed account of the 1936 poll results and methods will be found in "Public Opinion Polls" by Daniel Katz and Hadley Cantril, *Sociometry*, 1937, vol. 1, pp. 155–179.

7. The public opinion archive we created was the only one of its type in the world at the time. I felt it was of the utmost importance to preserve the punched cards and the codes of as many surveys done by other groups as we could get our hands on, since those who conducted the surveys were not certain they could afford the cost of preserving and housing the rapidly expanding material. The proper files for the cards were expensive and the men then doing the research could hardly be expected to spend their hard-earned money for essentially academic reasons.

The initial basis of the Archive consisted of all data gathered by Gallup and his American Institute of Public Opinion. Later we added to this the surveys of the National Opinion Research Center, the British Institute of Public Opinion, and all surveys done by the Office of War Information. Parenthetically, it might be mentioned that during this period I helped my friend, Harry Field, create the National Opinion Research Center by having a number of meetings with Mr. Marshall Field II and his lawyer, Louis Weiss. As a result, Mr. Field put up enough money to establish the first nonprofit survey organization able to do research for organizations working in the public interest. I suggested to Harry Field that he also invite Gordon Allport, social psychologist at Harvard, and Samuel Stouffer, then professor of sociology at Chicago, to serve as trustees.

To jump ahead chronologically, it occurred to me after the war that it would be extremely valuable if all the results of public opinion research could be carefully indexed and published in a single volume. Accordingly, funds were again obtained from the Rockefeller Foundation for this special purpose and, under the able management of Mrs. Mildred Strunk, a huge tome of 1,191 pages, indexing and reporting the results of public opinion surveys from 1935 to 1946, was published as *Public Opinion: 1935–1946,* ed. Hadley Cantril (Princeton University Press, 1951).

After 1945, survey research organizations so proliferated all over the world that I saw if I tried to keep up with them and maintain a complete archive, I would be doing little else and would risk being sidetracked from systematic social psychology. I therefore helped to set up an arrangement whereby the World Association of Public Opinion Research, through an initial grant from UNESCO, took over all the material we had accumulated since the publication of our big index. It was hoped that this work could be maintained in some European center where labor costs, especially those of translation, were lower than in America. The index of public opinion data we started has been continued by the Steinmetz Institute for Maintaining Accessible Files on Existing Social Science Research Data of the University of Amsterdam and is being published in their international review, *Polls.*

I was also delighted when Elmo Roper provided funds to Williams College to create a center to accumulate public opinion research results. The Roper Center, under the direction of a former student of mine, Dr. Philip K. Hastings, received all our Princeton archives, codes, and files to help them get started.

While the archives were at Princeton they were used by dozens of scholars, who had special tabulations of the data run for their own purposes. Most of the visitors were psychologists and sociologists, some were economists. Oddly enough, not a single political scientist (except one graduate student) ever darkened the door of the Office of Public Opinion Research between 1940 and 1955.

8. Hadley Cantril (contributing editor), *Gauging Public Opinion* (Princeton University Press, 1944).

9. The description of how modern sampling works which follows was prepared by Paul Perry, President of the Gallup Organizations.

The first step in drawing a national sample is to group the population into a number of large geographic regions such as, in the United States, New England, the Middle Atlantic States, the Midwest, the South, and the West, and then within each region further group the population by city size categories. The population is thus divided into a number of regional city size classes known in sampling terminology as strata. Within each of these strata the sample may be further subdivided with some advantages but these (regions and city size) suffice for many general purposes. Ordinarily the part of the sample drawn from within each such grouping should be in the same proportion to the total sample as the population in the grouping is to the total population. The sample drawn will be distributed correctly by categories to the extent that the census population data are up to date. Currently, the United States Census Bureau provides intercensal estimates of the regional population totals which can be used to draw a new sample using such strata or to correct a sample using counts obtained in the 1960 census.

Another common method is to use regions as geographic strata and within regions to divide the population by metropolitan areas and counties. The metropolitan areas and counties are termed the primary sampling units, and a sample of these is drawn first. Within metropolitan areas and counties further stratification can be introduced.

Within the regional city size strata or the metropolitan areas and counties, the population can be arrayed by localities such as cities, towns, and townships. Localities are then selected at random. The selected localities are subdivided into small geographic areas, and a mathematically random sample of these small areas is drawn.

In a country such as the United States, with census figures available for small geographic units, area samples can be drawn easily. For example, in the larger cities (50,000 and over) the number of dwelling units is reported by individual blocks. In smaller cities and towns and townships, population statistics are available by census tracts and enumeration districts, which are small administrative units delineated for census purposes and are useful for sampling. Maps or aerial photographs are available to identify the boundaries of such areas.

In cities for which block statistics are reported, it is possible to draw quite small geographic areas which can be, in most cases, exactly identified by street boundaries. Within such areas one can either list all the dwelling units and draw a random sample of them from the list or from roughly equal segments of 10, 15, or 20 dwelling units in the area. The latter is probably the method now used most frequently. In a segment of such size it is a relatively simple matter to list all the dwelling units and draw a sample of individuals from all of them. This can be done by listing all of the occupants in each dwelling unit who have the characteristics desired (as, for example, men and women 21 and older), and making a random selection from within each household. Usually it is the practice to limit the draw to one person per household. This will introduce some bias (small households will be overrepresented and large households underrepresented), which can be counteracted by taking into account the number of adults in each sample dwelling unit.

Outside of cities for which block statistics are published, census tracts or enumeration districts are the smallest areal units which can be drawn in the United States using census population counts. In such areas small geographic units must be defined on maps, an estimate of size in terms of population made by field inspection for all such units (where practicable), a unit drawn taking into account its size, the unit segmented in the manner described for blocks above, a segment drawn, and individuals selected as previously indicated.

If one is in a country without such detailed census data, the problem of drawing an efficient sample is more difficult, and, for comparable sampling tolerances, larger samples would have to be drawn. Fairly accurate estimates of the distribution of the population (including the principal centers of population) by geographic regions can usually be made even in relatively undeveloped countries. Small areas can be delineated and drawn into the sample on the basis of estimates of population size. Once these small areas are selected, methods such as those already described, listing all households, enumerating all members of selected households, and selecting a member of the household, can be used.

To be sure that a sample is unbiased, each step in the selection procedure should be such that every individual in the population surveyed will have a chance of being drawn and that the probability of selection will be known. This requires specific procedures at each step which are too detailed to describe here, but may be found in any recent book on sampling methods.

10. *Gauging Public Opinion* (see Note 8), Chapter 12.

11. I have mentioned the nonprofit research corporation,

American Social Surveys, Inc., established to receive funds and carry out research. A note seems in order here about the usefulness and value of such nonprofit corporations to academicians, since difficulties often arise in making contracts with universities and in following university policies concerning the hiring and paying of the special personnel sometimes involved. Furthermore, if research is to be done abroad, universities may be (or were in those days) reluctant to assume some of the obligations and responsibilities entailed. Not many people in the academic world seem to know about the great freedom of movement such simple, informal organizational structures can provide for research.

American Social Surveys was the first of four different nonprofit corporations which I set up and which are mentioned in this volume, the others being The Research Council, Inc., The Institute for Associated Research, and our present Institute for International Social Research.

It is a relatively simple matter, legally, to set up such a corporation if its purpose is quite clear and aboveboard and if a few men of distinction can be persuaded to serve on the board of trustees. Today, of course, it takes a longer time to obtain the tax-exempt status than it did in 1940, because the tax-exempt status has been so misused that the Bureau of Internal Revenue has each time to make a detailed, time-consuming investigation of the corporation's intention. Obviously, if one is associated with a university, as I was, the corporation should be set up with the full knowledge and permission of the president or responsible financial officer.

But once the tax-exemption is obtained, one is in a position to accept quickly foundation, Government, or private funds, without fixed overhead costs, and to employ at once what people are required, for the time required, and at the salaries required. Also the possibility of making special arrangements with other experts and of arranging subcontracts with research organizations both in this country and abroad is greatly expedited. In the case of American Social Surveys, and some of the research done with Government funds under the aegis of The Research Council, there was the enormous advantage of not having to take any full-time Government position, remaining a completely free agent but at the same time, as an "expert consultant," having access to relevant classified information.

Any such nonprofit corporation would however, for me, lose its many advantages if it became too large or complex. It must be kept simple, with administrative details handled by a competent assistant, to allow the chief investigators full time for their research.

12. A more detailed story of the origin and operation of the Princeton Listening Center is given in the Preface of *Propaganda by Short Wave*, ed. Harwood L. Childs and John B. Whitton (Princeton University Press, 1942).

13. Gerard B. Lambert, *All Out of Step* (New York: Doubleday, 1956).

14. Some time in the middle of the war, the following exchange of letters occurred between Jerry Lambert and the President. Unfortunately, Lambert has not saved any of these letters and we have had to reconstruct the wording to the best of our memory. I am including this exchange of repartee only to reflect the fact that even in the middle of the war Roosevelt, like Churchill, took time out for a bit of humor.

New York Yacht Club

Dear Jerry:

You may have noticed that due to the war there is a bill before Congress that would do away with the yacht ensign. As you know, this is one of the oldest ensigns in the country and we are eager to retain it.

Since you are working in Washington, I thought you might know some important people who could help keep this legislation from going through and I would appreciate anything you could do.

With kind regards,

   (Signed)   George

George Roosevelt, Commodore

Dear Mr. President:

Enclosed is a letter from your cousin George about a bill in Congress that would do away with the yacht ensign.

George asks if I know any important people in Washington who might help prevent this. I don't, but I thought perhaps you would.

If there is anything you could do for George, I know he would appreciate it.

Sincerely,

   (Signed)   Gerard B. Lambert

The White House

Dear Jerry:

Please tell cousin George that if this bill comes to my desk, I will veto it.

With best regards,

   (Signed)   Franklin D. Roosevelt

15. Charts II and III were first published in *Gauging Public Opinion* (see Note 8), pp. 220–221; Charts IV and V in the *Public Opinion Quarterly,* 1948, vol. 12, pp. 38–39; and Chart VI in *The Annals of the American Academy of Political and Social Science,* 1942, vol. 220, p. 145.

The questions on which the trend charts are based were phrased as follows:

Charts I and II:

1. Which side do you think will win the war—England, or Germany and Italy?
2. Do you think the United States will go into the war in Europe some time before it is over, or do you think we will stay out of the war?

Chart III:

1. Which of these two things do you think is the more important for the United States to try to do—to keep out of war ourselves, or to help England win even at the risk of getting into the war?
2. If the question of the United States's going to war against Germany and Italy came up for a national vote within the next two or three weeks, would you vote to go into the war or to stay out of the war?
3. Do you think the United States should declare war on Germany and Italy and send our army and navy abroad to fight?
4. Do you think it was a mistake for the United States to enter the last World War?
5. Do you think the United States should risk war with Japan, if necessary, in order to keep Japan from taking the Dutch East Indies and Singapore?

Chart IV:

1. In general, do you approve or disapprove of the way Roosevelt is handling his job as President today?
2. In general, do you think the Government has gone too far or not far enough in asking people to make sacrifices for the war?
3. The way things are going right now, does it seem to you that we are winning the war or losing it?
4. If Hitler offered peace now to all countries on the basis

of not going further but of leaving matters as they are now, would you favor or oppose such a peace?

5. Do you feel that you have a clear idea of what this war is all about—that is, what we are fighting for?

6. If the German Army overthrew Hitler and then offered to stop the war and discuss peace terms with the Allies, would you favor or oppose accepting the offer of the German Army?

Chart V:

1. Do you think Russia can be trusted to cooperate with us when the war is over?

2. Which country is the greatest military threat to the United States—Germany or Japan?

3. Which of these two things do you think the United States should try to do when the war is over: Stay out of world affairs as much as it can, or take an active part in world affairs?

4. If Germany is defeated, do you think a peace that will last for at least fifty years can be worked out?

5. How much longer do you think the war with Germany will last?

6. How much longer do you think the war with Japan will last?

16. Winston Churchill, *Blood, Sweat, and Tears* (New York: Putnam, 1941), p. 348.

17. *New York Times*, May 19, 1944, p. 5.

18. *New York Times*, March 4, 1944, p. 1.

19. *Longer version of December 15, 1942, memorandum to the President.*

It is of prime importance that no step be overlooked to make sure that the Commander-in-Chief and the Government agencies under him hold the full and increasing confidence of the people.

The most powerful mediums for accomplishing this are the news given out about production and the news given out about the progress of the war. This memorandum is confined to the question of handling the news on production. If the principle recommended is agreed upon, the best way of applying it to war news can then be reviewed and planned.

Recommendation:

It is recommended that all statements, quotas, or predictions in reference to production of war materials in 1943 be so phrased that the figure finally, or periodically, achieved will surely exceed the original announcement. It is a deliberate policy of understatement and overperformance.

No country is so well prepared as the United States to take advantage of this policy, for we have not yet approached the peak of production, and even conservative quotas will represent a staggering achievement.

A prediction of 50,000 instruments of war followed by a final production of 45,000 instruments is a failure. But a prediction of 40,000 followed by a final result of 45,000 is a success. The production is the same—the difference is in the handling of the information.

In considering the proposal, it is important to remember that neither the people nor most Government officials have any way of knowing whether a quota is adequate or not.

The desired result can be obtained by the control and agreement of very few agencies. The White House, the War Production Board, and the Maritime Commission or War Shipping Administration almost cover the range of the problem.

If this policy is adopted, the results will be:

1. A sustained and firmly rooted confidence in the Commander-in-Chief and those under him, thus strengthening the hand of the Administration.

2. Discouragement of the enemy by the growing belief in our statements.

3. Elimination of a strong point in enemy propaganda, namely, failure to achieve production quotas.

4. Elimination of a point of criticism for opponents and legislative bodies.

It is a fallacy to urge that national total goals of production higher than can possibly be attained will lead to increased effort on the part of the worker.

High quotas in individual factories may still be used to accomplish maximum production, since individual productive units relate their own efforts to local quotas assigned to them.

Attached herewith are five charts derived from recent public opinion surveys pertinent to this subject.

Chart I shows that 26 per cent interviewed feel the President has not got production up to promises.

Chart II shows the amazing rise in optimism when the African campaign opened. Such wide swings are dangerous, and a policy of understatement should stabilize them.

Chart III is another illustration of the fact that the American public is volatile. It indicates the marked sensitivity of the people to a temporary military setback, Rommel's advance.

Chart IV shows that Americans are suspicious of exaggeration. Russian reports have destroyed confidence in their accuracy.

Chart V gives the results of a survey showing that half the people do not even remember the production announcements for 1943. This points out that conservative quotas for the coming year can safely be used. Although the public forgets the figures, the immediate danger lies in the probability that as the end of the year approaches, there will be a flood of reviews and post-mortems by the press, recalling the past predictions, and thus pointing out comparative failures.

Adoption of a policy of understatement requires immediate consultation with the leaders in charge of major activities and news policies—war production, shipping, and Office of War Information. No doubt they are at the moment preparing elaborate year-end, round-up stories on our results. A simple agreement on the principle will require only a change in a few figures.

It is better to make one clean-cut revision downward *now* than to be forced frequently throughout 1943 to explain why quotas were not attained.

It should be pointed out that the above recommendation deals only with the tangible realities of production, and in no way suggests a let-up in the drive to build up emotional enthusiasm for the war. On the contrary, the final result of this policy will be increased confidence in a successful outcome.

Do you think our production of ships, planes, and tanks has been as great as the President said it would be?

Yes	60%
No	26
Don't know	14

Per cent who believe Allies winning war

July 29, 1942	25%
Sept. 15, 1942	45
Oct. 27, 1942	36
Nov. 17, 1942	81

Per cent who think the British are not doing all they possibly can to win the war

May 21, 1942	28%
June 3, 1942	24
June 9, 1942	18
June 25, 1942	41
July 1, 1942	33
August 13, 1942	28
August 25, 1942	21

Confidence in news coming from Russia

Express doubts about its accuracy	47%
Express no doubts	53

Do people recall production estimates contained in the President's Message to Congress last January?

Do you remember how many planes the President said he thought we would build?

Remember	52%
Don't remember	48

How about tanks?

Remember	43%
Don't remember	57

How about tons of shipping?

Remember	43%
Don't remember	57

20. *Supporting data that speech should be conciliatory and that cooperation should exist.*

Question A:

In January the Congressmen elected in November will take their seats in Washington. Do you think this new

Congress should cooperate in every way possible with the President in his conduct of the war, or should Congress not let the President have as much say as he has had about the running of the war?

Cooperate	72%
Not let President have as much to say	18
No opinion	10

Question B:

In January the Congressmen elected in November will take their seats in Washington. Do you think the President should cooperate in every way possible with the desires of this Congress or should the President feel free to conduct the war the way he thinks best?

President should cooperate	72%
President feel free	28

Question C:

If Congress should disagree with the President on any major problem concerning national affairs or the conduct of the war, in general, do you think the President or Congress should have final authority?

President	58%
Congress	42

Question D:

If the President should disagree with Congress on any major problem concerning national affairs or the conduct of the war, in general, do you think Congress or the President should have final authority?

Congress	72%
President	28

21. *New York Times,* January 18, 1961, p. 1.

22. *New York Times,* March 18, 1942, p. 1.

23. *Ibid.*

24. Detailed figures on opinion toward the lend-lease bill and on lend-lease operations are given in *Public Opinion: 1935–1946* (see Note 7), pp. 409–415.

25. *New York Times,* November 12, 1943, p. 1.

26. *New York Times,* August 18, 1944, p. 1.

27. *Questions dealing with international cooperation.*

Most people think our Government is doing a good job of looking after our interests abroad. Only a quarter hold the view that other countries are taking advantage of us.

> "Do you think that this country's interests abroad are being well taken care of by the President and other Government officials, or do you think other countries are taking advantage of us?"

United States interests well taken care of	62%
Others take advantage of us	27
No opinion	11

The overwhelming majority of the American people want their Government to take steps *now* toward the establishment of a world organization.

> "Should the Government take steps *now*, before the end of the war, to set up with our Allies a world organization to maintain the future peace of the world?"

Should take steps now	81%
Wait until after war	11
Stay out always	8
Total in favor of world organization (now or after war)	92%

Some examples of public ignorance of United States foreign policy.

1. Less than half know United States was not a member of the League of Nations.

"Has the United States at any time been a member of the League of Nations?"

Yes, belonged	30%
Don't know	26
No, not member	44
Total ignorant	56%

2. Two-thirds are unaware of any Senate resolution on foreign policy.

"Have you heard or read about the resolution recently passed by the Senate on America's postwar international policy? This was called the Connally Resolution."

Have heard	34%
Have not heard	66

3. And two-thirds of those who *have heard* of the Connally Resolution think the United States will join an organization of nations after the war.

"As you understand this resolution, does it mean that the United States will join an organization of nations after the war?"

United States will join	64%
United States will not join	9
Don't know	27

28. *New York Times,* January 24, 1945, pp. 1, 4.
29. A review of American opinion on postwar problems

was prepared by Jerome S. Bruner when he was with us in the Office of Public Opinion Research during 1943–44 and was published in his book, *Mandate from the People* (New York: Duell, Sloan, and Pierce, 1944).

30. The more complete details of this study were published in the *Public Opinion Quarterly*, 1965, vol. 29, pp. 400–410. But I am deliberately including considerable detail also in this report, since the situation made it essential to adapt standard procedures and devise new techniques. Throughout the whole undertaking, the advice and assistance of Professor Leonard W. Doob, social psychologist at Yale University, then with the Psychological Warfare Branch of Military Intelligence, was most helpful.

31. Captain Harry C. Butcher, *My Three Years with Eisenhower* (New York: Simon and Schuster, 1946), p. 36f.

32. Winston Churchill, *The Hinge of Fate* (Boston: Houghton Mifflin Company, 1950), pp. 531–532.

33. *Supporting data concerning Administration's postwar policy.*

The questions asked, on which the charts were based, were:

> I want to find out how much interest you have in international affairs, such as setting up an organization of nations, supplying other countries with food, machinery, etc., and I want to compare this with your interest in home affairs, such as full employment, increased social security, etc.
>
> Please tell me first: How much interest do you have in *international affairs?* None at all, a little, a considerable amount, a very great interest, no answer?
>
> Now would you tell me how much interest you have in *domestic affairs*—that is, affairs here in the United

States? None at all, a little, a considerable amount, a very great interest, no answer?

The "average interest" indicated in the chart was calculated by simple weighting procedures.

Comparison of Public Interest in Domestic and International
Affairs

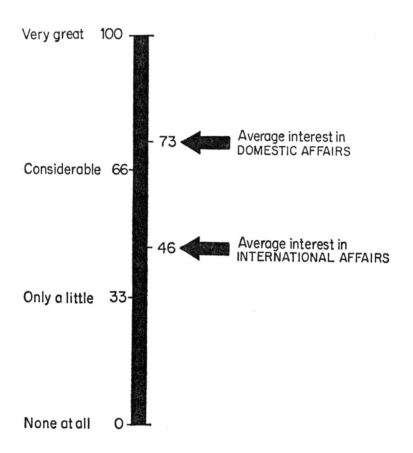

INTENSITY OF INTEREST

Very great 100

— 73 ← Average interest in DOMESTIC AFFAIRS

Considerable 66

— 46 ← Average interest in INTERNATIONAL AFFAIRS

Only a little 33

None at all 0

Interest in Domestic and International Affairs Compared in
Different Educational Groups

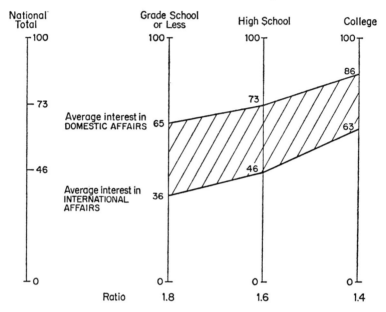

Estimated number of people in United States over 25 years
old in different educational groups:

Grade school or less	45,000,000
High school	22,000,000
College	7,000,000

Summary

1. The higher the education, the greater the interest in
   both domestic and international affairs.
2. The higher the education, the greater the comparative
   interest in international affairs.
3. The above results—considered numerically or in terms
   of votes—show the predominant concern of the 45 million at the lower end of the education scale with problems here at home.

If a candidate for President in 1944—either Democratic or Republican—made the following statements about what our policies should be after the war, which one would meet with your greatest approval?

We must give all necessary aid to friendly countries even at a good deal of sacrifice to ourselves	31%
We must not give so much aid to foreign countries that it will lower our standard of living here in this country	64
No opinion	5

If the United States does furnish all necessary aid to friendly countries after the war, what effect do you think this would have on our standard of living here at home—would it be raised, lowered, or stay about the same?

Raised	10%
Lowered	45
About same	31
No opinion	12
Qualified answer	2

34. *New York Times*, January 12, 1944, p. 12.

35. *New York Times*, December 21, 1964, in a dispatch headed EISENHOWER REGRETS POLICY OF TOTAL SURRENDER.

36. Wallace Carroll, *Persuade or Perish* (Boston: Houghton Mifflin, 1948). In this book, Mr. Carroll gives a detailed account of the problem and what was done about it (pp. 215–231).

37. *The appeals used in test of plausibility in Italy and Holland:*

1. *Peace.* The people of the world want peace. They know that another world war would be even more costly in terms of life and resources than the last war. And so

the people of Western Europe, including Italy (Holland), working with the United States under the Atlantic Pact, are determined to preserve the peace by making themselves so strong that the Soviet regime would not dare to carry out further aggression. They believe that, with things the way they are now, peace can only be assured if those who really want peace are strong.

2. *Individual dignity.* The final aim of government should be to uphold the dignity of the individual and to protect those freedoms which give all people the greatest chance to shape their own destinies. In order to work toward this goal, the nations of Western Europe, including Italy (Holland), have joined together with the United States into the Atlantic Pact Organization to protect themselves from those who have no respect for the sacredness of the individual and his rights.

3. *Soviet threat to independence.* It is evident from the aggressive policies the Soviet Union has already demonstrated in Czechoslovakia and Korea that the men who run the Soviet Union have no respect for the independence of nations. The nations of Europe might easily be conquered separately if they were left alone to defend themselves. For this reason, it is most important that all people in Western Europe join together with the United States through the Atlantic Pact so that the independence of each nation can be protected.

4. *Fear of United States domination.* With the United States rearming and urging the nations of Western Europe to rearm, it is only natural that many people in Italy (Holland) should fear that the United States wants to dominate the world and that Italy (Holland) may lose some independence by close cooperation with the United States. But the United States has no imperialistic motives and is interested only in preserving the freedom and in-

dependence of democratic nations, including its own. The nations of Western Europe should therefore not be afraid to cooperate with the United States through the Atlantic Pact Organization.

5. *Better tomorrow—general.* The people of Western Europe, including Italy (Holland), should be able to look forward to a time not too far off when they will have a higher standard of living, better pay, better housing, and greater security in their jobs. The United States has tried through such things as Marshall Plan aid and its Point Four program to help people everywhere to achieve this goal. But a brighter future would be threatened if Communism should spread over Italy (Holland), in spite of what the Communists are saying. If the people of Western Europe are to look forward to a better tomorrow, it is therefore important that they cooperate with the United States in the framework of the Atlantic Pact Organization to protect themselves.

6. *Better tomorrow—specific United States reference.* The United States knows that the standard of living of all its people—not just the privileged few—is higher than any place in the world. The United States would like to see the working people in other nations have the same job security, the same high pay, the same old-age and health benefits, the same rights for labor unions that its own working people have. In order that progress toward these goals shall not be stopped by those who would dominate all our lives if they came to power, the United States believes that it is to the great advantage of all nations of Western Europe, including Italy (Holland) as well as to its own advantage, for all to work together through the framework of the Atlantic Pact Organization.

7. *Become strong for self-interest.* It should be obvious from the actions of the Soviet Union in recent years that

if the nations of Western Europe, including Italy (Holland), do not do their utmost to make themselves strong they will soon be gobbled up by the Soviet Union. The self-interest of Italy (Holland) therefore clearly lies in the direction of cooperation with the United States, the strongest and richest nation on earth, in rearming through the Atlantic Pact Organization for common defense.

8. *National pride.* The people of Italy (Holland) have a right to be proud of their country, of its contributions to civilization in the past, and of its importance and responsibility now in world affairs. In order that Italy (Holland) may continue to play its important role as a nation for its own people and its historical role in the community of nations, Italy (Holland) must continue to do its utmost to cooperate with the United States and other European countries through the Atlantic Pact Organization.

9. *European Union.* The people of Western Europe, including Italy (Holland), are working with the United States through the Atlantic Pact Organization to rearm for common defense. The best way to speed this rearmament and to make the Atlantic Pact Organization really work would be for all democratic nations in Europe to join together in a European union and to have a single, common European army.

10. *Democracy—control.* The aim of the United States can be stated very simply: to strengthen democracy both within the United States and in other countries. Since the beginning of the United States as a nation, it has stood for freedom of the individual under a democratic government chosen by the people. To protect this way of life, the United States believes that all the democratic nations of Western Europe, including Italy (Holland), should cooperate with the United States through the Atlantic Pact

Organization in order to make themselves strong through rearmament.

11. *Europe must do more*—(control). Because of the heavy burdens the United States has carried since the war in giving billions of dollars to help other nations, in providing armaments abroad, in the fighting in Korea, it is now necessary that the nations of Western Europe, including Italy (Holland), carry more of the load of recovery and rearmament by redoubling their efforts immediately through the Atlantic Pact Organization.

38. Hadley Cantril, *The Politics of Despair* (see Note 4). This report is excerpted from Chapter 8, which had the title heading, "Words, Arguments, Appeals: Two Experiments." I am grateful to the original publishers for permission to reprint excerpts from this chapter.

All procedural details of the study are given in Appendix 3 of *The Politics of Despair* and need not be repeated here. These include the complete texts of the appeals used and a report of all the results obtained.

39. I reviewed the research plans during my tenure as director of the Tensions Project in the *Public Opinion Quarterly*, "The Human Sciences and World Peace," 1948, Vol. 12, pp. 236–242.

40. *Tensions that Cause Wars,* ed. Hadley Cantril (Urbana, Ill.: University of Illinois Press, 1950).

41. William Buchanan and Hadley Cantril, *How Nations See Each Other: A Study in Public Opinion* (Urbana, Ill.: University of Illinois Press, 1953).

42. A. N. Whitehead, *Modes of Thought* (New York: Macmillan, 1938), p. 119.

43. Hadley Cantril, *Soviet Leaders and Mastery Over Man* (New Brunswick, N.J.: Rutgers University Press, 1960).

44. Our impressions of Soviet psychology were written up

for our professional colleagues and published as "Some Glimpses of Soviet Psychology" (Mark May, Henry A. Murray, and Hadley Cantril) in *The American Psychologist,* 1959, vol. 14, pp. 303–307.

45. This research, including its systematic background, methods, results, and conclusions, is contained in Hadley Cantril, *The Pattern of Human Concerns* (see Note 2).

46. George F. Kennan, *On Dealing with the Communist World* (New York: Harper & Row, 1964), p. 18.

47. *A suggestion for gearing psychological dimensions into foreign policy considerations:*

(I am fully aware of the complications involved in trying to introduce into the machinery of Government some organizational effort that would guarantee that the psychological dimensions of foreign policy I consider so important would be taken into account. Perhaps my suggestion here may stimulate some experts in governmental procedures to a more workable solution. I have not attempted to draw any ideal organization chart. Many good men have been defeated by charts, and no chart can function in practice without a proper coordination of intelligence, teamwork, and absence of self-interest. I have perforce kept my suggestion brief, which means it is also somewhat abstract.)

1. A small group should be set up at the White House level, responsible directly to the President. This might be done best within the framework of the National Security Council; in any case, it should be intimately related to it. The objective of such a group should be to ensure that all foreign policy planning is based on a sound understanding of the psychological and political dynamics of the peoples involved. Careful consideration should also be given to the kind of information to be distributed to the American people, in order that they may understand the relevance of foreign policies to their own personal welfare.

(The advisory group suggested here differs in important aspects from previous organizations that have been established to handle comparable matters, such as the Psychological Warfare Board and the Operations Coordinating Board. These were *not* set up at the White House level and were *not* composed of full-time, experienced people from outside the Government with independent staffs of their own.)

2. All members of the group should be appointed by the President. The chairman should be a person who is known to have the complete confidence of the President. All members of the group should be persons who understand the way of thinking I have been describing, who have had some experience in applying it, and who have demonstrated professional competence. Once appointed, the group should try to keep itself as simple, informal, and flexible as possible.

3. The chairman of the group should maintain close relations with key policy-making groups, should attend meetings of the National Security Council, and keep in close touch with members of the cabinet. Only in this way can the group keep fully informed about problems as they emerge and be sure that Government decisions are made in the light of ideological and psychological considerations so that military, economic, and diplomatic action may have the maximum desired impact.

4. The group should have complete freedom of action, should have no administrative responsibilities, and should be on a full-time basis.

5. The group should keep in close touch with the Secretary of State, the Secretary of Defense, the Director of the Central Intelligence Agency, and especially the Director of the USIA, as well as with the heads of all other departments or agencies involved in explaining and disseminating United States policy objectives.

6. The group should have control over setting up its own methods of gathering information, as well as access to all Government information desired. The group should be free to commission research studies and analyses, both within the Government and in non-Governmental institutions and research organizations.

7. The group should have a relatively small but highly trained staff of experts, who should be able to draw on the facilities of Government agencies, who have considerable familiarity with various parts of the world and the domestic scene, and who are experienced in disseminating information or in research methods.

8. It would be a most important educational function of the group to devise ways and means of sensitizing the public, the Congress, and all Government personnel, from the President on down, to the psychological considerations required to make Government policy effective and to avoid its being set back by off-the-cuff and ill-timed remarks of prominent citizens or Government officials who talk before they think. Above all, the group must try to assure itself of ways and means to see that systematic data relevant to particular problems are marshalled together at the right time and flow without interruption to the key individuals responsible for final decisions.

9. The activities of the group, together with all recommendations accepted by the President, should be properly financed. The group should have funds of its own which it could, with the President's approval, disperse to operating agencies for essential programs and emergencies. Certainly the funds now appropriated annually for overall information purposes are picayune, given the job that needs doing. But the problem will never be solved merely by pouring more money into current programs, although many phases

of these programs clearly deserve greater financial aid. Whatever funds are appropriated should be periodically reviewed in terms of their demonstrated effectiveness. Only by some such system could Congress be expected to approve the appropriations required.

Index